TOO MUCH HORROR BUSINESS

TOO MUCH HORROR BUSINESS

THE KIRK HAMMETT COLLECTION

by KIRK HAMMETT

with STEFFAN CHIRAZI

ABRAMS IMAGE

EDITOR: David Cashion

INTERIOR DESIGNERS: Mark Abramson, Rose de Heer

CASE DESIGNERS: Kirk Hammett, Mark Abramson

PRODUCTION MANAGER: Ankur Ghosh

Library of Congress Cataloging-in-Publication Data

Hammett, Kirk.

 Too much horror business / Kirk Hammett.

   p. cm.

  ISBN 978-0-8109-9659-5 (hardback)

1. Horror films—Collectibles. 2. Motion pictures—Collectibles. 3.

Hammett, Kirk. I. Title.

 PN1995.9.C53H36 2012

 791.43'075—dc23

                          2012015629

Printed and bound in China

10 9 8 7 6 5 4 3 2

Abrams books are available at special discounts when purchased in quantity

for premiums and promotions as well as fund-raising or educational use.

Special editions can also be created to specification. For details, contact

specialmarkets@abramsbooks.com or the address below.

THE ART OF BOOKS SINCE 1949

115 West 18th Street
New York, NY 10011
www.abramsbooks.com

I want to dedicate this book

to my wife, Lani, and my two sons, Angel Ray and Vincenzo,

for their love, patience, and understanding,

and also to Chefela Hammett and Dennis Hammett (1937–2011)

TABLE OF CONTENTS

INTRODUCTION

From the Cave of the Unholy One

PART 1 – MOVIE POSTERS & PROPS

4   One Man's Obsession: A Conversation with Kirk Hammett, Part

18   Movie Posters & Props – 1920s

28   Movie Posters & Props – 1930s

48   Movie Posters & Props – 1940s

58   Movie Posters & Props – 1950s

78   Movie Posters & Props – 1960s

88   Movie Posters & Props – 1970s and Beyond

PART 2 – TOYS & MASKS

102   The Collectors: A Conversation with Kirk Hammett, Part 2

116   Toys – 1960s

148   Toys – 1970s

168   Masks

PART 3 – ARTWORK

180   Music & Monsters: A Conversation with Kirk Hammett, Part 3

192   Artwork

215   Credits & Acknowledgments

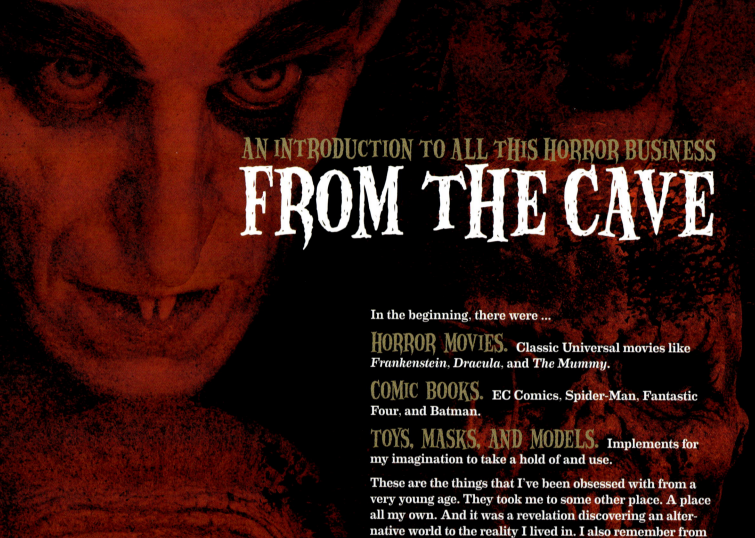

AN INTRODUCTION TO ALL THIS HORROR BUSINESS
FROM THE CAVE

In the beginning, there were ...

HORROR MOVIES. Classic Universal movies like *Frankenstein*, *Dracula*, and *The Mummy*.

COMIC BOOKS. EC Comics, Spider-Man, Fantastic Four, and Batman.

TOYS, MASKS, AND MODELS. Implements for my imagination to take a hold of and use.

These are the things that I've been obsessed with from a very young age. They took me to some other place. A place all my own. And it was a revelation discovering an alternative world to the reality I lived in. I also remember from the very beginning, feeling an immense sense of joy, pleasure, and excitement when I engaged myself in all of this.

Is it a bad thing? I don't think so. Is it wrong to be a dreamer? Some dreamers have changed the world! Is it wrong to surround yourself with reminders of where your mind has been and what your mind felt once it was there? No.

All throughout my life I've had to explain why I've had such an attraction to all this business, this horror business. And the simple explanation is ... it's fun! It's exciting for me. It comforts and relaxes me in a way that a sunset might relax any other person, except in my case it would be a full moon and some strange, malevolent creature lurking about!

My imagination has always been very active, which means I'm the kind of person who is never bored in even the most boring situations because all I've had to do is watch the ongoing movie in my head that is constantly teleporting me to an alternate reality. And the urge to

OF THE UNHOLY ONE

surround myself with tokens from this other reality feels perfectly natural to me. These tokens, whether they be posters, books, artwork, toys, music, comics, or the movies themselves, have always been a big source of inspiration in my daily life. And at one point, I became aware of the cultural significance of this, the fact that through this journey I have found myself taking for the last forty-four-odd years, I have managed to cobble together a rare old treasure trove of goodies. This fed another urge to bring the different aspects of this culture together, and to create a more distinct and clear picture of the history of all this horror business ... which brings us to the main point.

Too Much Horror Business is an attempt to compend the fruits of my labors into something tangible that I can share with like-minded enthusiasts — and I know you're out there, en masse! — the casually interested, and anyone who basically gives a shit!

Allow me two "slightly-insecure-so-must-clarify" nerd moments here. Firstly, the toy collection is by no means complete, there are numerous items that still need to be unearthed. The condition on some of these items range from "stone cold mint in the box" to "as is," and some of the latex props are just barely holding in there!!!

But the patina of age, while inevitable, can be interpretive, indecipherable, and lends its charm to many of the items found in these pages.

Secondly, there has been absolutely no attempt to intellectualize this subject matter in any way: leave that to the scholars! I have not seen every single movie referred to in this book (98% of them I have though! Ha!), and any lingering thoughts of stodgy intellectualism have been purposely blown away by my decision to do every single caption myself! By the way, please note that I don't list

what's a "half-sheet," "one-sheet," etc., in the '60s, '70s, and '80s Movie Posters & Props sections, because unlike the decades before, it's pretty damn obvious! Plus it would be really boring seeing "one-sheet," "half-sheet," "one-sheet" over and over! Well, it would be to me anyway! The main goal was to put it all together in an exciting and entertaining format that maximizes the inherent visual appeal of said items.

As should be screamingly clear by now, I've gone through decades living with this predicament, and it shows no signs of ever waning. Thank God!!!

People have tried to explain my curious "horror business" condition to me, telling me that I'm obsessive and compulsive with ADD and a hoarder. Maybe they're right, I don't know and I don't worry about it. Because to me, I'm simply a collector.

A keeper.
A curator.
A warden.
A historian.
A guardian.

Yeah, I am also a father, a musician, a surfer, a regular guy. But ask me about 1935's *The Black Cat*, and you will get a complete dissertation from me about the OBVIOUS merits of this classic movie at the drop of a hat!

Welcome to my world ... enjoy it!

ONE MAN'S OBSESSION

THE BIRTH OF A RABID COLLECTOR

A conversation
with Kirk Hammett

You will probably be able to tell more about Kirk Hammett from the collection you are about to see than any typical biographical text that could be conjured up. I have known Kirk for twenty-eight years, and he has always been wonderfully idiosyncratic and dreamily obsessed with monsters, ghouls, toys, movies, and guitars. He is a shy person by nature, but mention *Creature from the Black Lagoon* or *The Mummy* or *Famous Monsters* magazine and his eyes literally widen, his spirit opens up, and you'd be advised to settle in for a long and enthusiastic conversation. He is, in many ways, like a rock 'n' roll Edward Scissorhands who has managed to cultivate a comfortable world to live in.

That world, which stands aside from rock 'n' roll and aside from Metallica and aside from Lani, Angel, and Enzo, is made up of one of the world's finest collections of horror memorabilia. There are posters, toys, masks, artifacts, and stacks of collectible treasure that serve at once to satisfy a burning desire to acquire and curate, while also keeping Hammett firmly in touch with the brightest and most comforting aspects of his childhood. Those same movies, toys, magazines, and artifacts were firm friends to the younger Hammett, glorious avenues of escape from a world that was sometimes confusing and cold.

Too Much Horror Business is primarily about the collection Kirk has amassed, but by mere nature of the reason for its existence, it is also autobiographical. Which is why Kirk and I decided to present three conversations: one about childhood, another on the nature of collecting, and a final one on how music and horror have worked together in his life. They are presented in a simple Q&A format, and were conducted in Hammett's San Francisco home and a Parisian hotel room during 2011. And by talking with him about the movie posters, the toys, the props, and the world of a collector, you will learn more about Kirk Hammett than perhaps he ever knew about himself!

So, without further ado …

Steffan Chirazi
January 2012

SC When do you first remember being scared of something horror-related?

KH When I was five years old I got into a fight with my younger sister and managed to sprain my arm. My parents then said that I couldn't go outside and play, that I had to just calm down and relax. Which meant that they did what most parents did during the '60s, they sat me in front of the television, and I soon found myself watching this movie called *Day of the Triffids*, which is about gigantic man-eating plants. And you know what I remember the most? Watching that movie, getting really, really scared, yet trying to draw these triffids that scared me so much. I

was obviously as fascinated as I was scared by them. I realized that *Day of the Triffids* was a *different* kind of movie. It gave me *another* sense, *another* feeling. And I enjoyed this "other feeling" very, very much.

SC Why is it that you identified with these sorts of movies whilst so young?

KH I think they made me feel something that the other movies I'd watched had not. They gave me a sense of self-awareness that I had previously not felt, a feeling of mortality and reality that Disney films and children films did not give me. I would watch these "other" films and pretend I was in scenarios. I would be a monster that was bound by rope and I was breaking out, "the outcast" fighting back. I suppose that's how I felt deep down, and these movies were the ones that started to help me, in some way, know it.

My room and the streets became places to play these games in my head. I'd coerce people into them, too, when I could. My sister never went for it, but I had younger cousins I managed to get into these games.

I would be the monster chasing them, you know. I would be the monster breaking out and terrorizing everyone. I remember very, very vividly seeing my brother bring home an Aurora monster model of Frankenstein soon after I'd seen *Day of the Triffids*. I didn't know exactly what it was, but I was aware that it was a monster movie because I had seen pictures or stills somewhere. It made an enormous impression on me. Two monster heads came with the model. My brother painted one head as realistically as possible, and my cousin—he probably doesn't even remember this—painted the other monster head, giving it a psychedelic spin. It was green, it was orange, it was blue, it was yellow, it was red, it was pink, it was purple.

SC We should perhaps point out that this was all during the sprawling cultural explosion that was flower power versus Vietnam and the late 1960s peace-and-love era.

KH Yeah, and what my cousin had done was totally of the time, because both him and my brother were involved in the whole hippie scene with Haight and Fillmore, all of that good stuff. Which gives you a basic view of my early childhood, worshipping my brother and my two cousins. They were my heroes. And I would hang on every single word that they said. All three of them were in college at the time, and again, this was the hippie era, so they were going to the Fillmore and the Avalon Ballroom, to all these free concerts in Golden Gate Park and whatnot. So not just horror business, but the music business was brewing in my head as well.

SC What would you say was the most interesting result of being with them and being introduced to all this counterculture goodness?

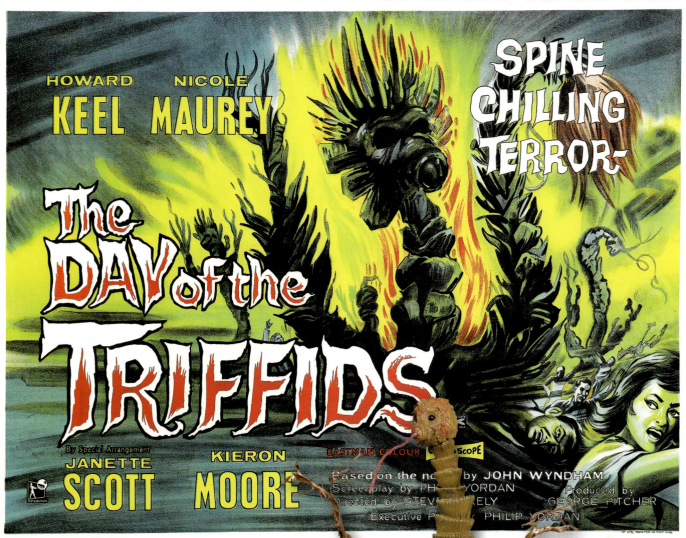

THE DAY OF THE TRIFFIDS

The Day of the Triffids took over my mind! These frightening flora really scared me when I was a wee lad. It's laughable how back then I thought walking plants could be so menacing! The poster is a British quad.

KH The most interesting by-product of all this stuff was how I very quickly came to recognize, and gravitate to, things that were horror-related, as if I'd always had it inside and just been waiting for the catalyst. I had another cousin who brought over a full, proper over-the-head Wolf Man mask, and I was obsessed with it. I remember putting it on and all of a sudden feeling this huge sense of power, like I had stepped into another sort of existence. I was someone else. And I remember just feeling how supercool that was. I was a monster. And my cousin would then pretend that he was scared, just for my amusement. But the feeling! ... It stuck. It was deeply engaging and addictive in its own way.

SC What did your parents think about all this developing monster and movie passion?

KH It was strange in a way because all the while, Mr. and Mrs. Hammett hadn't noticed what was happening to young Kirk. They just glanced around and wrote it off as "Kirk acting funny and being goofy" or whatever. But I was *fine* not being recognized, because it allowed me to carry on digging deeper into this intriguing world. My parents started to give me milk money, twenty-five cents a day, which was enough to get some milk and a donut, ten cents for the milk, fifteen cents for the donut. And I remember getting the money, going to school, looking at the donut and the milk and saying, "I don't think I'm gonna buy those today." Instead, I went to a newsstand that was a couple blocks away from my house and bought a comic book. And that comic book was the *Fantastic Four.* And I loved it, even though I could barely read it. I was five and a half years old and already in first grade because my parents put me in school early, so I was always the youngest kid in class, which came with its own unique set of problems. However, there I was, five and a half with disposable income!

I had suddenly figured out that saving that quarter a day gave me access to a world I wanted to know intimately. That feeling intensified when I went to a local newsstand and saw a horror magazine, *Creepy.* I couldn't believe my eyes! *Creepy* magazine was a bunch of stories put into a magazine format, which allowed it to get around a "censorship board" called the

Comics Code. They were around in the '50s, '60s, and '70s, and basically they mandated that comics couldn't show violence along the lines of, say, stabbing someone with a knife, or axing someone, or having a stake through the heart, or seeing someone with their head split open—nothing like that was allowed in comics. *But,* if it was put into magazine form? Fine! And so I bought my first issue of *Creepy* magazine and it really blew me away, especially the stories, which were still in comic book form but were technically in a "magazine." There were three magazines like that, *Creepy, Eerie,* plus the more photo and movie-oriented *Famous Monsters of Filmland.* The other magazine of this ilk I used to read was *The Monster Times.*

SC Do you think that going to a Catholic school in the Mission District of the city helped somehow encourage this developing passion of yours?

KH Oh yeah, I have little doubt that going to a Catholic school and being taught by the sisters plays into all this somewhere, somehow. Even going to school was a daily journey of escape. It was a three-block walk alone to school, and on the way I'd do what I mentioned earlier and turn the streets into a game, an imaginary world where everyone was playing roles. I'd look up at all the people going by and imagine that one guy was a monster, and another guy was a mad scientist, sometimes ducking behind mailboxes or whatever, depending on where my imagination took me. I'd scare myself sometimes, but that was the point, to feel that feeling and enjoy it, even though I had no idea what it really was or why it made me feel like it did.

After school, the idea was to go straight to my house, and then walk from there to the comic store. Not to even stop and take off my little Catholic school uniform. I would just unbutton my shirt so it would be open, have a T-shirt

CREEPY AND THE MONSTER TIMES

Two epic magazine covers from my youth!

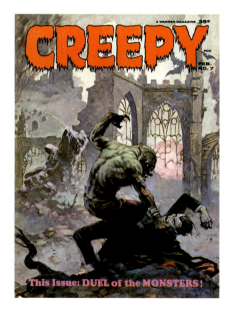

The large photo here was made from a negative I found, and it appears to be an outtake from the photo session for *Famous Monsters #2*, circa 1958. Dig that suit!

underneath, and walk quickly to the comic book store.
I remember the day I had enough money to buy a
Famous Monsters of Filmland magazine. I remember the
exact issue, and I actually have the original cover-art painting, which is Boris Karloff as the mummy. But I mostly
remember getting it and being drowned by this overwhelming feeling of excitement, and so it would be the
moment that I'd say I was hooked. Because even at that
young age, it had become a lifestyle: saving milk money to
buy monster magazines.

SC Did this developing passion interfere with school in
any way?

KH Of course! Unsurprisingly, because these magazines
became so important to me, I started bringing them to
school in the second grade and showing them to all my
friends. A few of them were into it, but most of them were
decidedly not. And my second grade teacher started taking the magazines away because I not only had them in
school, I was reading them during class. Which wasn't so
good, really. This led to my second grade teacher coming
to the house to meet my parents. She proceeded to say that
"Kirk's a really good student and if he could just learn to
put away the monster mags and comic books he's gonna
really, really, really, do well in school." I still remember
thinking, "Yeah, OK, if those are the choices then I know
what mine is gonna be!" I was also a pretty popular kid
in that I was "different," I was "weird." I was the kid who
always had monster magazines in class, and I was the kid
who was always talking about movies. So as I traveled
from grade to grade with the same group of thirty kids,
from first grade all the way to seventh grade, my reputation as being "the monster kid" was pretty big. Friends
would come up to me and say, "Hey, did you see the monster movie on Creature Features last weekend. What did
you think?" which was cool.

SC At a certain point, your mom must've known you
were not buying milk and donuts....

KH Well, yes, soon my mom realized that I was spending my milk and donut money on monster magazines, but
she'd still ask, "Where'd you get that?" so I told her the
truth. I told her I'd found a store four blocks away that sold
these magazines, and that I really like the magazines. And
probably because she was just proud of the fact I was reading at five or six years old, she didn't say much else about
it. She also saw that I really loved monster movies, so she
would actually start telling me when certain movies were
gonna be on TV. So she was actively encouraging this interest, which felt really great even though I couldn't articu-
late that at the time.

SC And your father?

KH Once my father *realized* I was into all this stuff, he'd
take me to the movies. We saw *The Green Slime*, a sci-fi
horror flick, together, and he also took me to *2001: A Space
Odyssey* when it first came out. I suppose my whole family
could see my obsession from an early age. My brother took
me to see *Barbarella*, because it had a GP rating [GP was
the old PG] and you had to be accompanied by an "elder,"
as Jane Fonda had that zero gravity nude scene. And boy,
when I saw that! ... I was just a little horndog kid! So then
it became "Yeah, boobies! Aliens! Cool!" This all led to
my discovering a movie theater on 23rd and Mission, the
Grand Theater, where they had these weekend matinees
on Saturday and Sunday, three horror flicks for a quarter.
They attracted every kid in the neighborhood, and I was

one of those eager viewers. It was thanks to these matinees that I was exposed to a life-changing series of films: *Night of the Blood Beast, Bucket of Blood, The Abominable Dr. Phibes, The Texas Chainsaw Massacre, House on Haunted Hill.* These movies grabbed me, shook me, and never let me go. I loved them. I loved the extremity of them, the monsters, the look, all of it.

SC   An entire generation or few has really been cheated by not enjoying the Saturday matinee picture extravaganzas. I think it's such a shame.

KH   Oh yeah, totally. I saw a lot of great, great stuff. It wasn't only horror films, they'd also show movies like *Shaft, Super Fly,* and also I particularly remember all the *Planet of the Apes* movies being shown when I was a little older. They'd do these "festivals" and, boy, were they fun. Things like a Bruce Lee festival, where you'd get *Chinese Connection, Fists of Fury,* and *Enter the Dragon* in one sitting.

I also remember the Ray Harryhausen films, like *Golden Voyage of Sinbad,* with its stop-motion animatronic skeleton fighters, which blew my mind. It was just so cool, so out of this world to me. It was the same thing with the Hercules movies. They were super-cheesy, but they were also so great because they just went for it, they tried to capture the exact vibe of the stories and didn't let technology (or relative lack of) stop them. I loved them for bringing many of the things I was already seeing in the monster magazines to life. This is all why, from second grade to about seventh grade, all I lived for were the monster magazines, comic books, all the related toys, seeing Creature Features on channel 2, nine o'clock Saturday nights, and those Saturday and Sunday matinees.

SC   Did you buddy-up with friends when you went to the movies?

KH   No, not really. I know that going to the movies is seen as something you do with company, but oftentimes I would go alone because none of my friends could handle seeing two or three movies, whereas for me, the escape was wonderful. Things at home were often strange.... You have to understand, this was the '60s and early '70s in San Francisco, it was the hippie generation with its freethinking, liberal approach to life. And my parents had a lot of hippie friends who would come over, they would drink and act funny, which was a lot for a boy to take on board. Later on I figured out that hallucinogenic drugs had definitely entered the equation, that's what everyone was doing back then, plus my father drank a lot. So for me, watching Creature Features was a chance to get away from what all the grown-ups were up to. I would sequester myself in the TV room and watch my monster movies. And then during the day, a lot of times on Sunday during the matinees, I would get out of the house to the theater because there would be these people hanging around who I didn't really know. So as well as being fully into the entertainment aspect, this was my way to create an alternate reality for myself.

SC   So this whole passion sprung as much from a need to find a "world" to "escape to" as simple, idle enjoyment?

KH   Well, I used to pretend I was a monster, and that people around me were monsters. And then there was my getting engrossed in comic books. I used to look in the back pages of the comics and monster mags at all the little things they sold, wanting them. Obviously I was too young to think of it as collecting, I just wanted to wear the mask or play with the toy. But I'd see these cool Don Post masks in the back of the magazines, which had a price tag of $35, and back then, to me, that might as well have been $3,500. It was just as unattainable.

This was also a time when I would go down to the store, go shopping with my mom, and beg her to buy me a monster model. And then I *finally* started getting an allowance of a dollar, which was *only* given if I did all my weekly chores. But back then, a dollar could get you a comic book, a movie matinee, a soda or some candy, and maybe even a toy.

SC   What was the first monster you really connected with, the one who rocked your young world?

KH   It was the original *Frankenstein,* the one with Boris Karloff. When I heard it was on one night, I sprinted into the TV room to watch it. My father watched it with me, and he was saying what a fantastic job Boris Karloff did playing the monster, how otherworldly the Frankenstein monster was. I then remember him jutting out his arms straight ahead, doing that Frankenstein impression we've all done. And then later on, I remember him saying something along the lines of "Man, that's such a great movie when you're stoned." I knew exactly what he was talking about, but I didn't care, as it went right over my head and anyway, I was more interested in monsters and that movie in particular.

SC   So your dad introduced you to your favorite monster. Cheap psychiatrists would speculate ...

KH   There's a lot of melancholy in *Frankenstein,* and he is the ultimate outsider who's also perhaps misunderstood. And the ironic thing about it is that throughout the course of the movie, the monster's trying to connect with his creator. He's looking for a father figure. And maybe for me, with the relationship between my father and I not being as strong as it could have been, maybe that's why this particular movie, and monster, made such a strong impact on me and is still one of my favorite movies. Perhaps I always deep down recognized it as something of a mirror for my world.

MARTIAL ARTS AND BLAXPLOITATION

These films are some of my favorites to this day. Ron O'Neal ("Super Fly") was a big influence on my sense of fashion. Bruce Lee was someone every kid looked up to in the '70s, and when I wasn't watching monster films I was watching either kung fu or blaxploitation stuff!

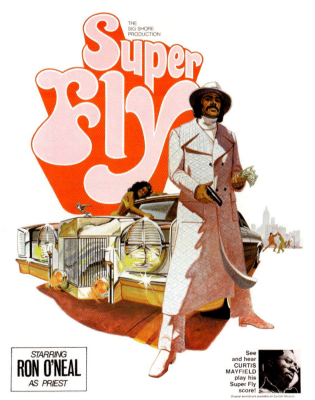

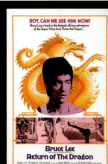

SC Which monster was next?

KH I loved all the Godzilla movies. Who doesn't want to see a sixty-foot-tall lizard tromping a city and swatting away jets like flies? That just kicked ass! And add King Kong to that list, too! Looking back now, I think it was empowering for me to see the outsider getting his way, even if it was just temporarily. Because, I was just a little kid who didn't have much control in my household. And I was afraid I might grow up to be like the little skinny guy in those Charles Atlas ads, the one getting sand kicked in his face. I wonder how many kids were traumatized by that ad?!

SC When you lay it out like that, the whole attraction of this world makes a lot of sense. What got you into the toys? Was it just a natural progression without too much over-thought?

KH I think so, sure. The very first monster model that I bought was a Frankenstein, and, like I mentioned earlier, my brother and cousin had earlier bought the same model, built it up, and painted it in a psychedelic way. It was the one with two separate heads, a regular and a glow in the dark, and at that point they were called Frightening Lightning kits. After watching my cousin paint one in these psychedelic colors, I thought, "That's not what these monsters look like!" So I felt compelled to buy a kit myself, and paint it true to my belief and perception of what Frankenstein's monster looked like. I wanted that model to be accurate, to be the pure vision of what the Frankenstein monster was, and more than that, I wanted it to be real, to be alive! I would go to bed early so that I could sit there in the dark and stare at the glow-in-the-dark models. And eventually, I saw all the main Universal monster movies like *The Mummy, Dracula, Wolf Man.* So I used to pretend that my monster toys were real. And, being like any other typical boy, I used to act on them a lot. A lot of the toys I have in my collection are toys I once had as a kid, but either blew up with firecrackers, set on fire, threw off the roof, drowned, buried, or whatever. In San Francisco, every July the whole place just became a fireworks celebration. I don't know about now, but back in the '70s it was very easy to get firecrackers. I used to know what sidewalk stands to go to in Chinatown to get all sorts of different fireworks year-round. I would get a few packs of firecrackers, put one in the Phantom of the Opera's hand, light it, run away, and watch it get blown up. And a week later I'd buy the same model again, rebuild it, repaint it, but this time I might set it on fire, or drop a big rock on it.

SC Let's discuss the comic book store, as it is a pivotal part of your ... *Horror Business.*

KH So I met a man called Gary Arlington when I was six, and he had one of the very first comic book stores arguably in the country, and maybe even the world, the San Francisco Comic Book Company. You have to understand, a store dedicated only to selling comics was totally abstract at that time.

His store was on 23rd and Mission, so very close to where I lived and right in my neighborhood....

You know, I tell people he was my surrogate father, and I learned a lot of things from Gary because whenever I had questions about any of this stuff, I'd go to him. So I basically learned about comics, vintage comics, buying and selling comics, trading comics, monster magazines, and everything else from him. And you know, as a little kid I would just sit there and wait for the right time to ask him a question about some comic book that was in a sleeve, up on the wall.

SC So Gary was one of your first idols?

KH Yeah, he was an idol of mine. He definitely had a sense of humor; he was a very funny guy. I would be staring at that monster magazine and say something like, "Wow, that's a really cool monster magazine," quite innocently. And then I'd say it again maybe ten minutes later because there might not have been a reply. So Gary would then reply, "What are you trying to say, Kirk? You know, you have to ask me things, not just drop hints. Ask and you shall receive!" He was always handing down little snippets of wisdom like that, which to a six-year-old was a big deal. Plus, his shop always had cool people in it. I saw underground comic book artists like Robert Crumb and Gilbert Shelton, which obviously didn't mean much to me then, but now, when I look back, I think, "Wow."

SC Did he ever give you any breaks?

KH Oh, he gave me lots of breaks because I was the kid who would not go away! I was the kid who was constantly pestering the adults in the comic stores, asking them questions about the comics they were buying or selling, asking them about Golden Age Captain America or whatever. Or I'd ask about a particular artist, like Neal Adams, Frank Frazetta, or Steve Ditko. I would basically sit there while all the other adult comic nerds talked shop and absorb it all. One time I was with my friend, who was stealing tons of comic books, and Gary suddenly called him over. He lifted up my friend's shirt and he had ten comic books shoved halfway down the front of his pants. He just said to my friend that he wasn't allowed in there anymore, and he said to me I was basically grounded from going to the store for a week!

And as soon as that week was done, I remember going there at 11:20 in the morning and waiting because they didn't open till twelve noon, on account of them being a buncha hippies! And once twelve noon came, there was Gary walking up, going, "Ha, ha, ha," opening up the door,

Gary's comic book shop was in San Francisco's Mission District, my neighborhood when I was a kid. I used to hang out at his shop, waiting for the new batch of monster mags to show up!

and letting me in like nothing had happened! I had that kind of relationship with him. He looked after me and did the right thing.

SC So you quickly became a young comic book nerd.

KH I was, but before the term was invented. Other comic book collectors as young as I was—six, when I really started—were pretty rare. There was a special place in my room for comics, I had stacks and stacks of them, which was obviously a key reason my mom figured out I wasn't spending that milk and donut money on milk and donuts! But what's interesting, when I look back, is that when I first started to trade stuff, it was usually because I wanted to start collecting something completely different.

SC So what's this about collecting from such an early age? I mean, that's the six-cent question we have to ask.

KH I've always felt like I had to be a curator and that I had to bring certain things together and put 'em in my space. Just to color my life with, to fill it with stories and images that inspire me. It was all part of controlling my world. I didn't have to deal with the reality of the outside world when I was in my room and reading comic books. I was totally creating and controlling my reality.

SC I'd like to talk about the role of religion in your young life, specifically in terms of its imagery.

KH Around the fifth grade, my young brain realized that there was something that didn't quite ring right with Catholicism. All that dogma was just not for me. Too many rules. Too many conditions. Too many contradictions when it comes to heaven and hell. I'm sure conceptually a version of heaven and a version of hell exist for everyone, but to me their version wasn't what I was seeing. So because of all this, I flunked religion in fifth grade. I got a big old fat F, the irony being, over time I have developed into a spiritual person, and someone who actually finds the concept of religion fascinating. Anyway, the nuns were not having it, but my mom said to me, "It's OK, Kirk, you believe what you want to believe." She wasn't one to push any sort of ideals or beliefs too heavily on my sister and I. The main reason I'd gone to a Catholic school, I think, was that they had a vested interest in my getting a good education.

SC As you sat in those churches, your mind was not on the Bible I suspect.

KH I was in church thinking of *Curse of the Demon,* and *The Wolf Man.* I was thinking of *The Mummy* and Egyptian culture. I was thinking of Greek mythology, and of Sinbad. I was thinking of witchcraft and *The Exorcist,* you know? *The Exorcist* resonated a little bit more because, hey! It's a Catholic thing!

SC There's some pretty violent imagery in churches, if one thinks about it.

KH Well, the whole Crucifixion scenario is very violent. I mean, especially for a kid!

I remember when I was three or four years old, I knew where my mom kept her Bible. I would take it off the shelf, open it up to the color plates, bypass all the stuff about the birth of Christ and the apostles, and go straight to the Crucifixion because that's what was cool, man, was seeing all the blood and gore. One of the color plates was Jesus being nailed on the cross. And I remember looking at that, holding up my little hand and going, "Uh, that's kinda scary," but being attracted to that. By the same token, my dad had a copy of Picasso's *Weeping Woman* on the wall, and I remember being very young, looking at that, and thinking that was a monster, too.

Looking back, as a kid there always seemed to have been daunting images everywhere I looked, so I suppose this horror fascination was pretty inevitable when you think about it.

WILLIAM PETER BLATTY'S

THE EXORCIST

Directed by WILLIAM FRIEDKIN

Something almost beyond comprehension is happening to a girl on this street, in this house ...and a man has been sent for as a last resort. This man is The Exorcist.

ELLEN BURSTYN · MAX VON SYDOW · LEE J. COBB
KITTY WINN · JACK MacGOWRAN · JASON MILLER as Father Karras
LINDA BLAIR as Regan · Produced by WILLIAM PETER BLATTY
Executive Producer NOEL MARSHALL · Screenplay by WILLIAM PETER BLATTY based on his novel

From Warner Bros. A Warner Communications Company

R RESTRICTED Under 17 requires accompanying Parent or Adult Guardian

74/40

THE EXORCIST

THE EXORCIST

Hands down, the most frightening movie of
my youth. It shook my Catholic faith and made
me feel vulnerable to demonic possession
because of my religion at the time!

ONE MAN'S OBSESSION

A UNIVERSAL
PRODUCTION

MOVIE
POSTERS
& PROPS
1920s

THE CABINET OF DR. CALIGARI
German double-panel (right), American one-sheet (below), three lobby cards

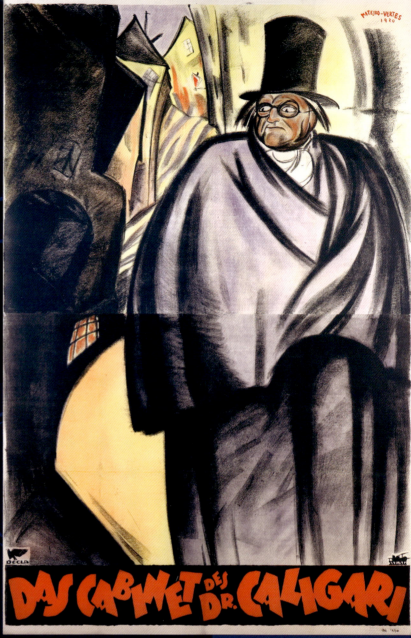

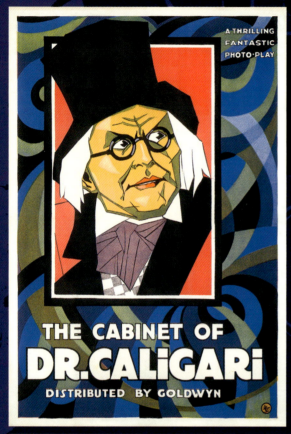

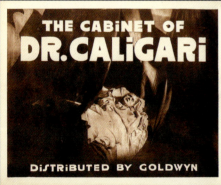

Created during the height of German Expressionism, *The Cabinet of Dr. Caligari* gives the impression of what it would be like if one was trapped in a spooky carnival show on a bad acid trip. Look at the lobby cards: the makeup on the sleepwalker (played by Conrad Veidt) was like a template for the goth rocker look! I particularly like the expressionistic look of the one-sheet poster with the psychedelic borders!

Der Golem is based on an old Jewish legend about a clay and stone automaton that, through alchemy, comes to life to save the Jewish people. Hollywood legend has it that Boris Karloff modeled his movements as the Frankenstein monster after the movements Paul Wegener used to play the Golem. I absolutely love the made-of-clay hairdo!

DER GOLEM
German double-panel,
American lobby cards

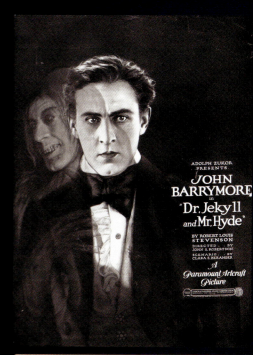

DR. JEKYLL AND MR. HYDE
Paramount Pictures print ad, French newspaper
photoplay edition

Classic silent film on the classic story, featuring
John Barrymore. In this version, Dr. Jekyll
looks very suave, whereas Mr. Hyde looks
very much like an unwashed hippie! Perfect
dichotomy!

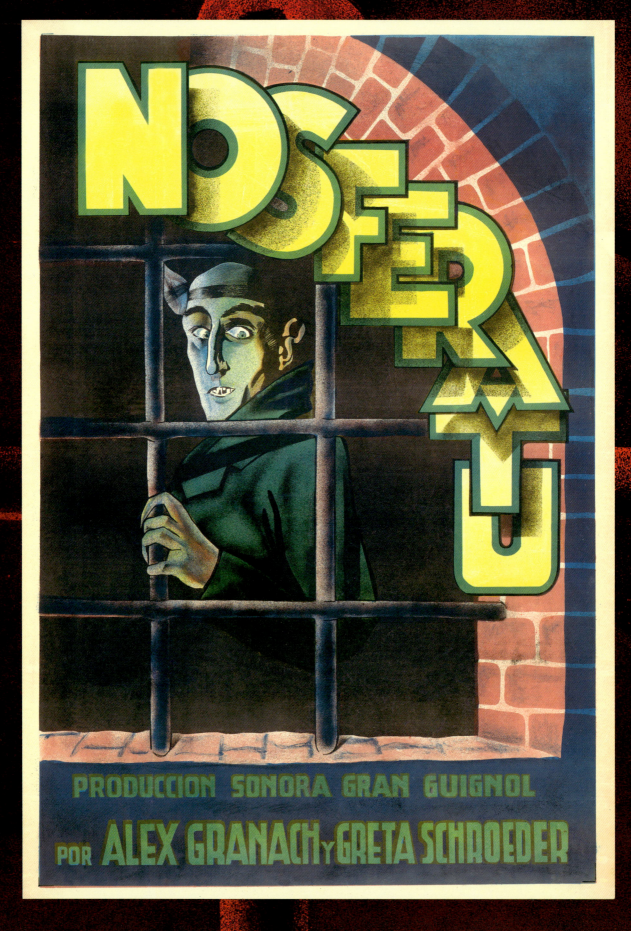

NOSFERATU *Spanish one-sheet*

Subtitled "A Symphony of Horror," this movie lives up to the music! *Nosferatu* to this day is still effective in giving me chills ... Eerie and atmospheric. Max Shreck is absolutely convincing as the undead. This one-of-a-kind one-sheet poster is my all-time favorite piece. I love the expressionistic rendering of Count Orloff with the three-dimensional art deco lettering. It frames the demented look on Orloff's face perfectly and gives the viewer a glimpse of pure evil.

HAMLET

Shakespeare would have loved this poster, and the fact that the part of Hamlet would be played by Asta Nielsen, a female actress! Extremely moody piece.

FAUST

American one-sheet

Movie on the classic Goethe novel. I love how the '20s always depicted the devil as a moustached actor in a red suit or robe with horns.

THE MAGICIAN/THE BAT

Lobby cards

In *The Magician* the protagonist seeks a fair maiden's virginal blood for his evil experiment. A common objective amongst my group of friends in high school, as I remember. *The Bat*, with a vibe very similar to *The Old Dark House*, is about people searching for a cache of money while being terrorized by a villain called the Bat. This character supposedly inspired Bob Kane to create his hero Batman.

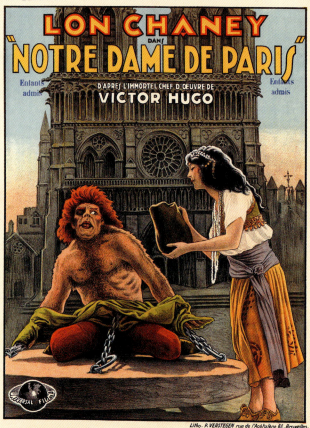

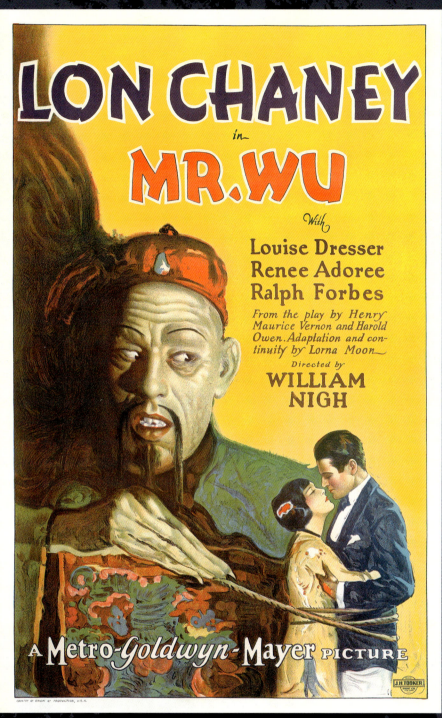

HIS FACE RINGS A BELL

Poor Quasimodo, he was just *sooo* misunderstood. Lon Chaney, the "Man of a Thousand Faces," was a true renaissance man. In *The Hunchback of Notre Dame*, Chaney did all his own makeup and stunts. Watching him swing from bell towers and ropes throughout the film just puts me in wonderment. The Belgian poster is particularly great. It shows my favorite scene in the movie, when Esmeralda gives the tortured and thirsty Quasimodo a drink of water.

In *The Phantom of the Opera*, Chaney becomes the face that launched a million nightmares! More than eighty years later and no one has yet come up with a more terrifying portrayal of the Phantom than Chaney. Through his mastery of makeup he created a movie character that the studio was reluctant to show pictures of in its promotional materials because his image was deemed "too horrifying." When the movie ended all I wanted to do was to become a makeup man. Thankfully, my hearing of Hendrix playing the "Star-Spangled Banner" soon changed that vocational aspiration.

The beautiful stone litho one-sheet from *Mr. Wu* features yet another great Lon Chaney role.

THE HUNCHBACK OF NOTRE DAME *Belgian one-sheet, American lobby cards*

THE PHANTOM OF THE OPERA *American one-sheet, lobby cards*

MR. WU *American one-sheet, Spanish heralds*

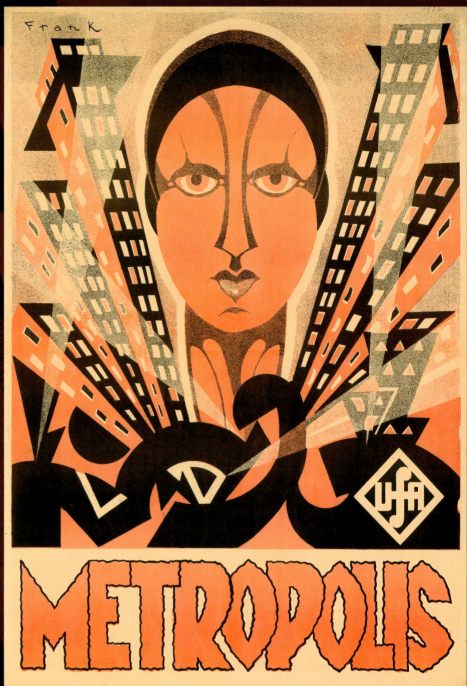

Every piece of movie material that I've seen on this very prophetic. incredible. and seminal science-fiction film has an interesting interpretation of what they created — a "vintage futurism look" that captivated me. The movie's theme relating to a culture of haves and have-nots remains vital today. And the Maria robot in the film struck me as exactly what an evil art deco robot should look like. The things I could have done if I had one as a child!

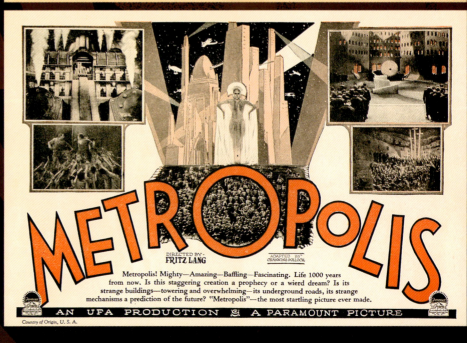

METROPOLIS
Opposite page: American insert. Swedish one-sheet. American print ad. This page, from top: German program, jumbo lobby card. American lobby cards

LONDON AFTER MIDNIGHT   *Argentine one-sheet*

I can't really tell you much about this film, because it is LOST. If you find it, contact me immediately! I think the last time it was shown was in the '50s, and no one has seen it since! Remade in 1935 as *Mark of the Vampire*, it's about a villainous hypnotist (Chaney) posing as a vampire. Chaney's vampire makeup, while different than what many might consider a "traditional" look for a vampire, is one of my favorite images in classic horror. If only you could see some of my Halloween costumes over the years! The stone litho one-sheet is an absolutely stunning piece, but this is one example where the film is actually rarer than the poster.

MOVIE
POSTERS
& PROPS
1930s

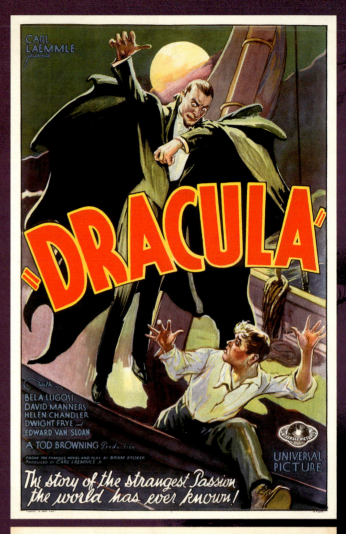

**DR. JEKYLL
AND MR. HYDE**
*American one-sheet,
Belgian one-sheet,
Australian daybill*

This is the definitive version of
Robert Louis Stevenson's classic
story. Fredric March won the Best
Actor Oscar for his incredible
performance, balancing just the right amount of sophistication
and poise with violence and outright insanity. His transformation
to Mr. Hyde at the hands of makeup wizard Wally Westmore
created an omnipresent suspense on the screen. Considering the
lustful, leering expression of Mr. Hyde when in the presence of
female company, it's amazing that it got by the censors of the time!

DRACULA
Opposite page: U.S. one-sheet, title card, two jumbo lobby cards. This page: U.S. one-sheet, insert, four lobby cards

The Story of the Strangest passion the world has ever known!

DRACULA

A TOD BROWNING Production — UNIVERSAL PICTURE — Presented by CARL LAEMMLE

CARL LAEMMLE presents

DRACULA

the story of the strangest passion the world has ever known.

with
BELA LUGOSI
DAVID MANNERS
HELEN CHANDLER
DWIGHT FRYE
EDWARD VAN SLOAN

A TOD BROWNING Production

Produced by CARL LAEMMLE Jr. A UNIVERSAL PICTURE from the famous novel by BRAM STOKER

Now here was a man who had a thirst for wealth and (human) taste! Hands down, Bela Lugosi was the best Dracula in my book (well, it is my book!). He had such a strong visual presence onscreen that it made me wonder if he actually believed he was a vampire. Because after watching the movie at age six, I believed he was a vampire! The movie material from this film is some of the most beautiful from the '30s, and the spiderweb motif is very effective (in the movie he walks through a spiderweb without disturbing it!). The lurid eyes on the one-sheet remind me of a pair of women's breasts, and in every picture he is poised to totally dominate his victims. One interesting thing I've noticed about Lugosi's portrayal is that, as suspenseful as it is, you never get to see his vampire fangs, they are merely suggested. It isn't until afterward that you realize you've not seen one drop of blood throughout the entire film. A true classic. Tod Browning's direction is chilling and the stark atmosphere, created by the lack of music, to this day influences my attitude toward dynamics as a musician and a songwriter.

IT'S ALWAYS BEEN ABOUT THE MONSTER!

Dr. Frankenstein's creation has always had a compelling effect on me. As a child I always felt like an outsider, so it was easy for me to relate to the monster's condition of loneliness and sorrow, and to how abandoned he felt in his quest to be understood. After all, he didn't ask to be created this way! The one-sheet pictured here looks like an Andy Warhol portrait gone evil. It is, in essence, an amazing example of pop art, thirty years before that term and movement were even invented!

The massive French double-panel poster dominates any room it is in. The funeral scene projects an overwhelming sense of impending doom. It was printed with a credit for the film's original director, Robert Florey, as well as James Whale, the director who replaced Florey before actual production began. Jack Pierce's makeup design, including the rather unique idea of the monster having a flat head, now stands as the unofficial trademark of Dr. Frankenstein's creation.

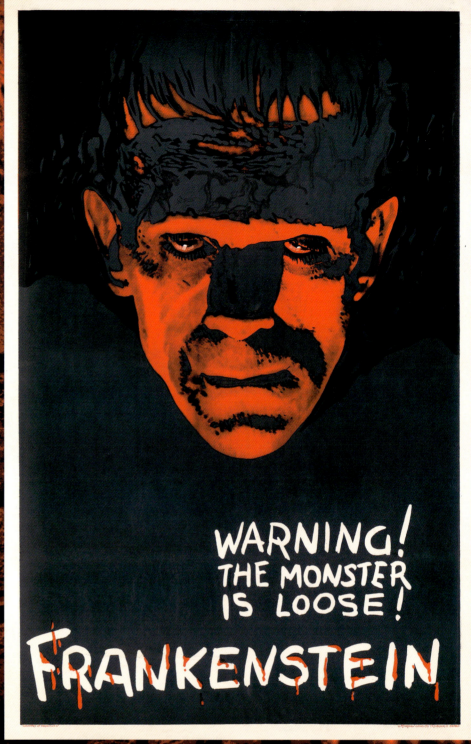

FRANKENSTEIN

Opposite page: U.S. one-sheet teaser, two lobby cards. This page: French double-panel, Argentine one-sheet, Australian daybill, U.S. one-sheet

THE MUMMY

This page: U.S. three-sheet
Opposite page: two U.S. one-sheets

The first twelve minutes of this film
was so burningly intense for me as
a child, it still holds its impact for me
now. The makeup Jack Pierce did for
Karloff's dual role as the mummified
Im Ho Tep and the present-day
Im Ho Tep are extraordinary! The
B-style one-sheet in the lower right
is the image we used to design what
is widely considered to be my most
popular guitar.

MUMMY DEAREST

It's all about Frankenstein's monster,
Dracula, and the mummy — the big three for
me! Since I couldn't honestly pick any one of
these classics flicks as my favorite, I decided
to design a guitar for each of them. Like the
movies, the guitars each came out looking
fantastic. But unlike the movies, the mummy
guitar has emerged as my favorite. Not only
does it look killer but it sounds killer, too!

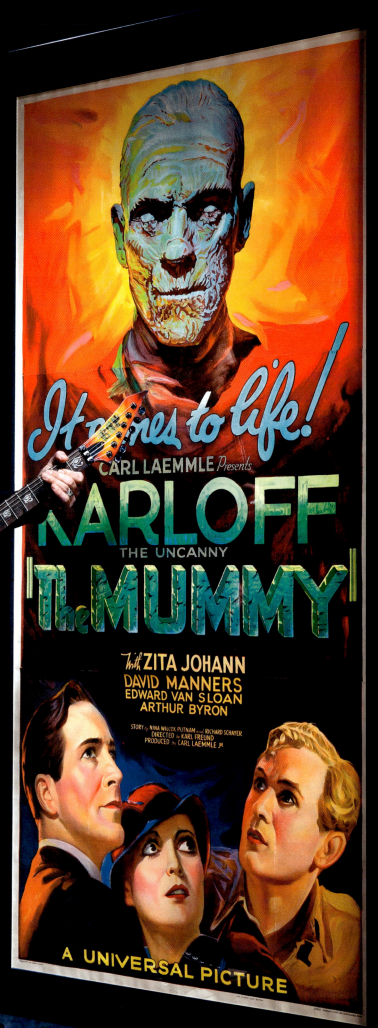

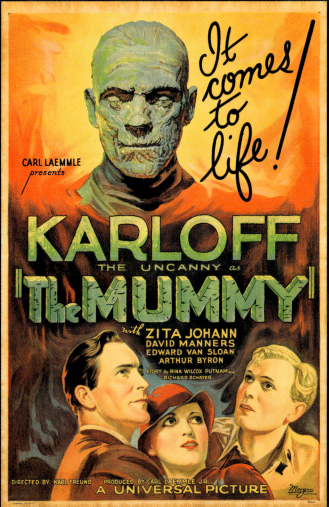

The Mask of Fu Manchu is a violent and crazed movie. Karloff's portrayal of Fu Manchu is sadistic and insightful, as he wields a death ray while wearing a mask of Genghis Khan. The lab equipment was created by Kenneth Strickfaden, a 1930s master of electrical effects. *Freaks* was the movie that threw Tod Browning's career into a tailspin. His decision to use real carnival performers was clever, but a little too much for audiences in the '30s.

**THE OLD
DARK HOUSE**
U.S. one-sheet, insert

Some have said this of my
house, at least until the kids
arrived with about a million
LEGOs and Tonka trucks.
In the flick, Karloff is billed
by his last name only,
signifying his stature at
the time as a heavyweight
actor. The one-sheet image,
of the terrified Gloria
Stuart with a looming
Karloff, remains one of my
favorites of this era.

VAMPYR
*Extremely rare original
concept art for movie poster*

DOCTOR X
U.S. one-sheet

MURDERS IN THE ZOO
U.S. one-sheet

Atwill had the X-factor!
Lionel Atwill had the heavy
demeanor and presence
that lent itself naturally
to horror movies, and
especially to villians. In
Doctor X he played the evil
scientist while in *Murders
in the Zoo* he was the crazed
zookeeper.

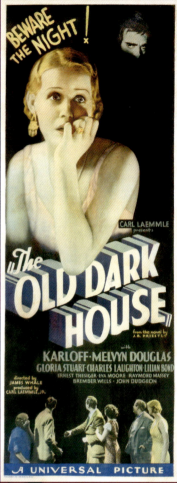

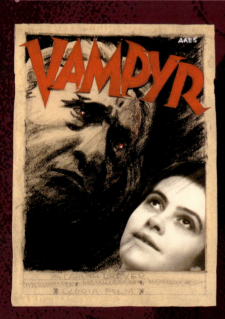

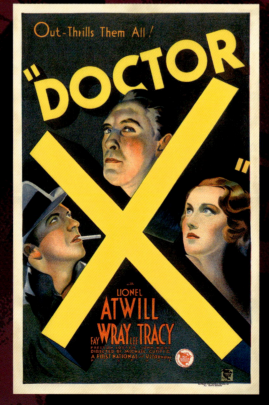

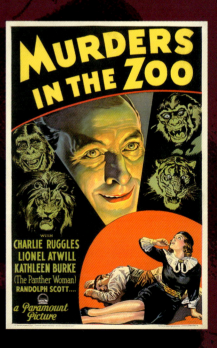

WHITE ZOMBIE
U.S. half-sheet, two lobby cards. The silicone Bela above is wearing the original vest and jacket from the movie.

With a title like *White Zombie*, and Bela Lugosi as a character named Murder Legendre, how can you go wrong? As the very first full-length zombie feature, this movie really took full advantage of Lugosi's thespian strengths as a villain, and his hypnotic screen presence. It was a common practice, back in the studio days of motion pictures, to use the same sets, props, and actors in as many movies as possible. If you look closely at the lobby card on the right, that is the same movie set that *Dracula* was filmed on.

THE MOST DANGEROUS GAME
Window card, two lobby cards, mounted head prop

Count Zaroff and his henchman live on an island where they hunt "the most dangerous game," and from the mounted heads seen on the lobby cards, you can deduce what that might be. This movie was filmed on the same sets used for *King Kong*. The prop is one of the mounted heads used in the film. You can clearly see which one it is on the posters shown here!

THE MYSTERY
OF THE WAX
MUSEUM
U.S. one-sheet

MURDERS
IN THE RUE
MORGUE
*Window card,
two lobby cards*

I love the
malevolence of
Dr. Mirakle, the
monobrowed
character Lugosi
plays in this
adaptation of Edgar
Allan Poe's story.

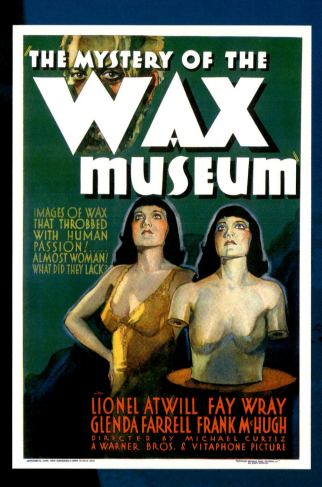

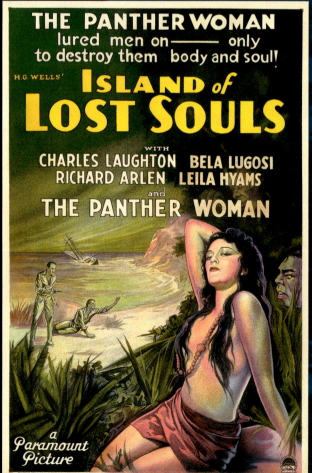

ISLAND OF LOST SOULS *Four lobby cards. U.S. one-sheet*

"Have you not forgotten the house of pain." screams Bela Lugosi,
the manimal known as the "sayer of the law!" The manimals were
the result of a crazy hybrid experiment. half-animal. half-human
creatures created by the evil and sadistic Dr. Moreau. This was one of
the greatest roles Charles Laughton ever played. I am always surprised
at how graphic this film was — with themes of rape. bestiality.
vivisection. and an underlying struggle of science vs. religion — given
that it came out in 1933.

KING KONG   *U.S. six-sheet. four lobby cards*

Typically six-sheet posters are the rarest of the rare given their massive size and limited distribution. What's even more odd about this particular poster is the image the producers chose to use to market the film. While much of the promotional materials focused on Kong on the Empire State Building with the girl. this image focuses on the most violent scene in the movie. What better visual to greet my friends when they come by the house for dinner!

THE GHOUL
British three-sheet, lobby card, Japanese one-sheet

Creepy, atmospheric British horror film that was lost for a while until a copy was found in the Czech Republic. Karloff plays a practitioner of alchemy and the occult.

THE VAMPIRE BAT
Two lobby cards

Made as a quickie sandwiched in between *Doctor X* and *The Mystery of the Wax Museum.* Lionel Atwill again, at his crazed best.

SON OF KONG *Two one-sheets*

THE RETURN OF CHANDU *Six-sheet*

Another six-sheet, this example is stunning. The film, a twelve-part serial, is interesting in that Lugosi plays the hero rather than the bad guy. Even better are the insanely hokie cat costumes those guys are wearing!

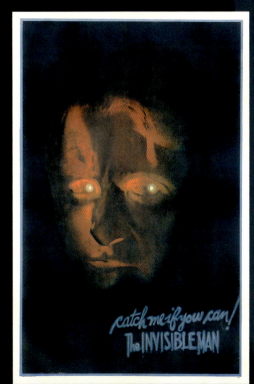

THE INVISIBLE MAN
U.S. one-sheet teaser, insert, half-sheet

This movie could be interpreted as some kind of pseudo-horror comedy. Una O'Connor is almost comedic in her nonstop screaming throughout the film! Question: Is the invisible man a nudist?

THE BRIDE OF
FRANKENSTEIN
*Clockwise from top: Snipe,
two U.S. one-sheets, insert,
lobby card, half-sheet*

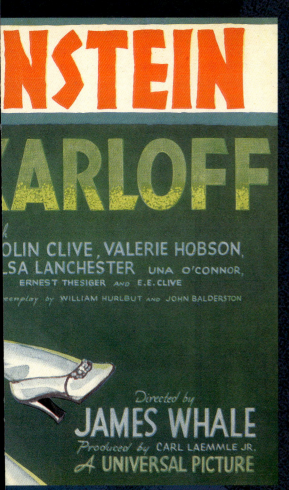

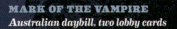

Like *The Invisible Man*, *The Bride of Frankenstein* is really a comedy in disguise. O'Connor's obsessive shrieking (again), the blind hermit teaching the monster to smoke, the crypt scene where Ernest Thesiger gets the monster drunk — this movie is hilarious! The ad department had a field day marketing this flick. The snipe at the top with the monster and his bride is totally over the top. The one-sheet above has an illustration of Elsa Lanchester.

MARK OF THE VAMPIRE
Australian daybill, two lobby cards

Carroll Borland is the classiest female vampire to grace the screen in all of the golden age of horror. Long black hair, dead white skin, shroud, and a ghostly stare that could see right through you! The best posters of this film are the ones that show her character, Luna. This film was a remake of *London After Midnight*.

MAD LOVE
Australian one-sheet, U.S. half-sheet, title card

This is an adaptation of a story called "Hands of Orlac," thus all the disembodied hands on the posters. One scene in this movie was so disturbing it gave me nightmares when I was a kid. Figure out for yourself which one it is! Items from this film are a rare commodity. Very little seems to exist today. The one-sheet and title card here came from

THE RAVEN
Belgian one-sheet,
U.S. half-sheet, lobby card

Karloff is a criminal who wants to change his identity and winds up disfigured by Lugosi, a doctor who collects devices of torture.

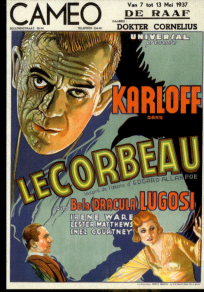

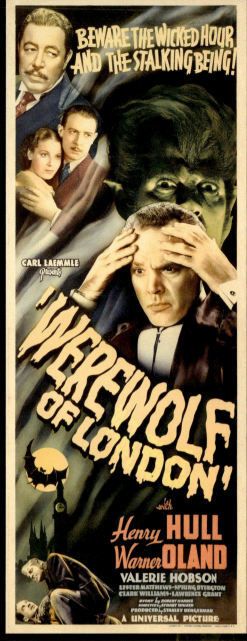

MURDER BY TELEVISION *Half-sheet*

A great title for an otherwise forgettable flick. I do like the shot of Lugosi on the half-sheet, which is vaguely reminiscent of a Transylvanian count. Or the maître d' at the Ivy.

WEREWOLF OF LONDON
U.S. insert, U.S. half-sheet

This was the first Universal horror movie to feature a werewolf, but he was a bit of a mad doctor when he wasn't howling at the moon. I love the notice on the half-sheet poster "To Hysterical Women! Shut Your Eyes!" So, did all the women miss the good scenes?

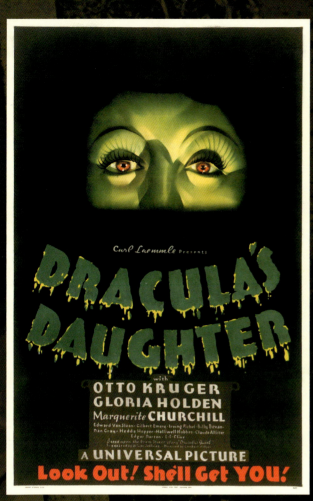

What is this weird feeling that she gives? It's that feeling that Lugosi should have been written into the script. The atmospheric six-sheet below is one of four Universal horror six-sheets known to exist. Some fog, a castle, a female vampire — perfect!

THE BLACK ROOM
Title card, two lobby cards

Karloff plays the role of twin brothers in this film. It's more like a mystery period piece than a horror movie. These lobby cards are very difficult to find, and a one-sheet poster has never been found.

THE INVISIBLE RAY
U.S. one-sheet, U.S. half-sheet, French double-panel

Another Karloff/Lugosi vehicle, this time Karloff has radiation poisoning and glows throughout the movie! The one-sheet has Karloff looking like the '30s pulp hero the Shadow.

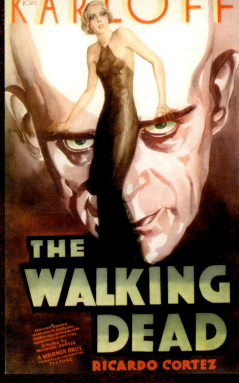

THE WALKING DEAD
U.S. half-sheet, U.S. one-sheet, two lobby cards

He must have had a long night! I love the art deco styling of these two posters, even though Karloff looks nothing like this in the film.

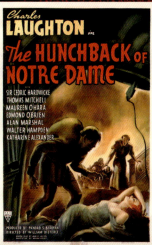

THE HUNCHBACK OF NOTRE DAME
U.S. one-sheet, French grande

Another version of Victor Hugo's classic story, this time with Charles Laughton. Not as dramatic as the Lon Chaney version, this adaptation is much more sympathetic to the hunchback than the silent film.

SON OF FRANKENSTEIN
Two U.S. one-sheets, three lobby cards, U.S. three-sheet

This third installment of the Frankenstein series is often overlooked, but in my opinion, this film is just as great! Lugosi turns in a great performance as Igor, the twisted hunchback, who was hung and declared dead, but miraculously survived to find the monster and wreak his revenge on the people responsible for his suffering.

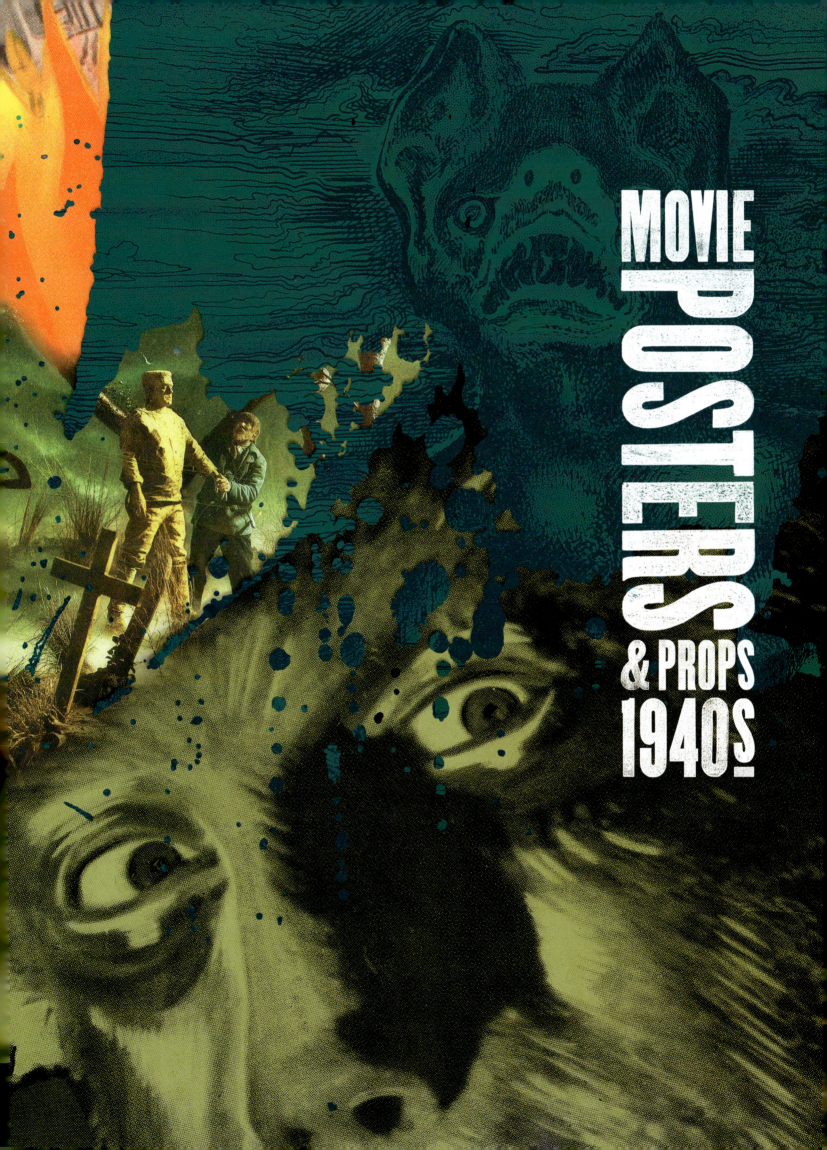

MOVIE POSTERS & PROPS 1940s

THE MUMMY'S
HAND
Lobby card,
U.S. half-sheet,
U.S. one-sheet

THE MUMMY'S
TOMB
U.S. half-sheet,
U.S. one-sheet

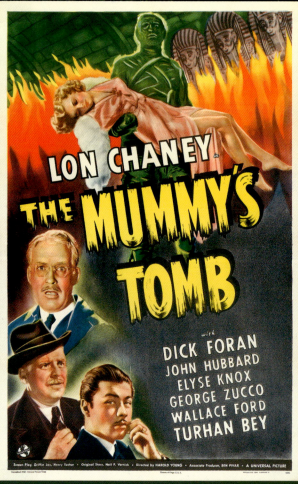

The Mummy's Hand was the first in the Mummy series of films, and has absolutely nothing to do with the 1932 film starring Boris Karloff. Tom Tyler, an actor known for his cowboy roles, played Kharis the mummy, who drinks tana leaf tea for sustenance.

The Mummy's Tomb was the beginning of Lon Chaney, Jr.'s role as the mummy. Legend has it that he hated having to sit through four hours of makeup for his role as Kharis.

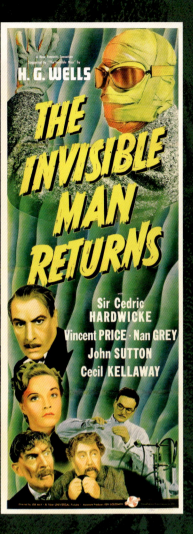

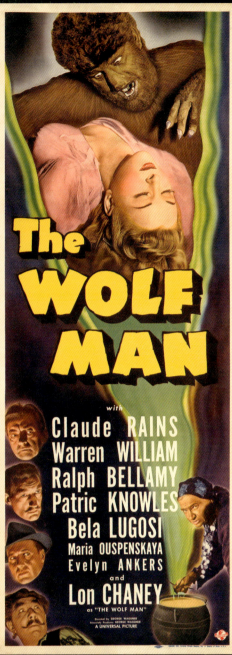

THE WOLF MAN
Insert, U.S. one-sheet, U.S. half-sheet, two lobby cards

The Wolf Man is a movie I can always relate to: sometimes when I go out when the moon is full I turn into a beast of sorts. The insert makes me laugh. It looks like the Wolf Man is gonna help himself to some breast meat!

THE INVISIBLE MAN RETURNS
Insert

Great image of the Invisible Man on this insert. This was Vincent Price's first horror film!

NIGHT MONSTER
U.S. one-sheet

Very atmospheric movie poster of this film, which gives Lugosi star billing even though he plays a very minor role.

THE GHOST OF FRANKENSTEIN
Insert, four lobby cards

PHANTOM OF THE OPERA *Title card, insert*

Claude Rains's portrayal of the Phantom is very spooky. I've always thought the Phantom's mask in this adaptation was the coolest looking of all the different versions.

CAT PEOPLE *Insert*

BLACK FRIDAY *Insert*

I've always noticed how similar the plot of this movie is to *The Ghost of Frankenstein* — the transplanting of brains into different bodies.

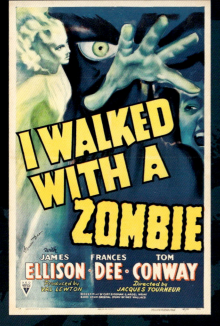

I WALKED WITH A ZOMBIE *U.S. one-sheet*

This poster is stunning. I really dig the eye and reaching hand, although zombies from the '40s were pretty tame compared to what we see today!

CALLING DR. DEATH *U.S. one-sheet*

SON OF DRACULA
U.S. one-sheet, half-sheet

I really enjoyed Lon Chaney, Jr.'s portrayal of Drac's son, Count "Alucard" (Dracula backward). The one-sheet cracks me up — it looks like ol' Alucard is about to cop a feel!

FRANKENSTEIN MEETS THE WOLF MAN
U.S. one-sheet

Very cool image on this poster of the monster and Wolf Man duking it out. This is actually a sequel to both *The Ghost of Frankenstein* AND *The Wolf Man*. Bela Lugosi finally got to play Frankenstein's monster in this film, after initially turning down an offer to play the monster in the first film.

THE HOUSE OF FRANKENSTEIN

Lobby card, half-sheet, one-sheet

A frightening faction of fiends! Universal decided five monsters were better than one, and proceeded to pack this film chock-full of them! This was the first film with Glenn Strange as the Frankenstein monster, and I feel his portrayal was second only to Karloff's!

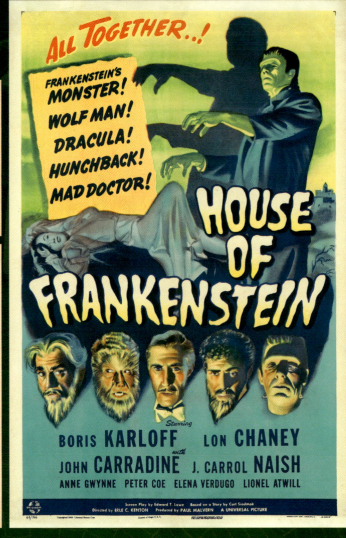

THE RETURN OF THE VAMPIRE

Insert, one-sheet, lobby card, props

This one-sheet has a great illustration of Lugosi that looks like Dracula, but is actually a two-hundred-year-old vampire named Armand Tesla. The props above are featured at the end of the movie when Tesla is destroyed by sunlight. On the left is Tesla's head before he starts to decompose, and on the right is his skull after the sunlight burned off all his flesh.

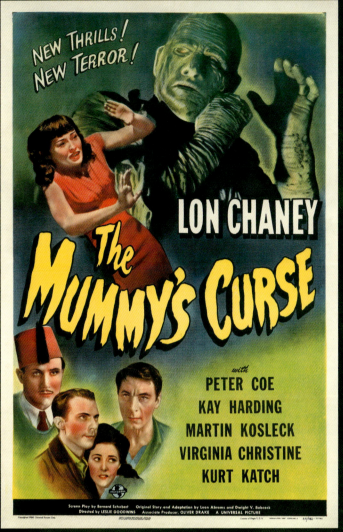

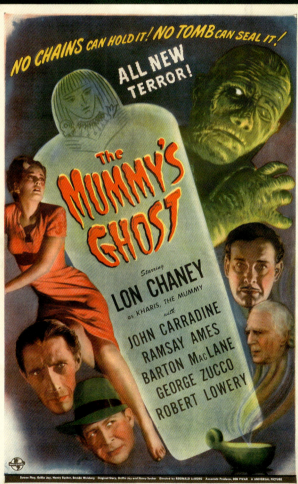

The image of the mummy is great on the posters from both *The Mummy's Ghost* and *The Mummy's Curse*, with the mummy's one good eye peering away. In fact, you'll probably notice that the mummy art on *The Mummy's Curse* posters is just a mirror image of the art on the *The Mummy's Ghost* posters. There is one sequence in the beginning of *The Mummy's Ghost* when the Egyptian princess rises from the swamp — that might be the best moment in any of these '40s mummy movies!

HOUSE OF DRACULA
One-sheet, insert, two lobby cards

This time the party's at Drac's!
Another monster rally movie,
this time with a beautiful
hunchback nurse! The insert is
particularly cool, almost like the
monsters are in a pop band and
this was their promotional shot!

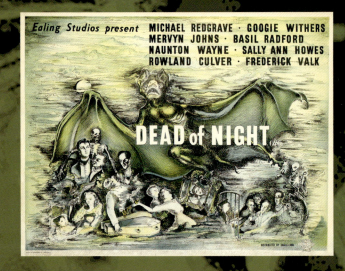

**DEAD
OF NIGHT**
British quad

**THE BEAUTY
AND THE BEAST**
French grande

**THE CURSE OF
THE CAT PEOPLE**
Title card

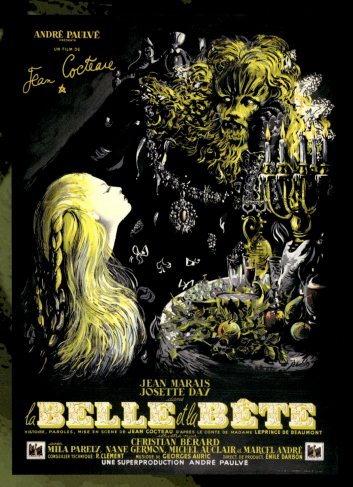

BUD ABBOTT AND LOU COSTELLO MEET FRANKENSTEIN
One-sheet, British quad, props

This was the last of Universal's monster rally films, and a personal favorite of mine. It was also the last time Lugosi would play Dracula, and Glenn Strange the Frankenstein monster. The British poster has a different title and graphics from its American counterpart.

The prop masks shown to the left are the actual papier mâché masks from the film, made by Emile LaVigne for Bud and Lou to wear to a costume ball. The Wolf Man bust below was a makeup test Bud Westmore created for Lon Chaney's role as the Wolf Man in the film, and the hanging cage from *The Black Cat* makes an appearance here as well!

...CRAWLING TERROR

THE THING *U.S. half-sheet*

THE DAY THE EARTH STOOD STILL *Insert*

Klaatu barada nikto! was something I used to say quite often as a kid. The quote is from Klaatu, Michael Rennie's extraterrestrial character in *The Day the Earth Stood Still*, one of my all-time favorite sci-fi movies! I wanted to have a Gort, too! The '50s started off with an atomic explosion with these three classic sci-fi movies, all featuring ominous alien beings. The apocalyptic vision shown on these posters makes for stunning artwork, especially in the case of *The Day the Earth Stood Still* and *The War of the Worlds*.

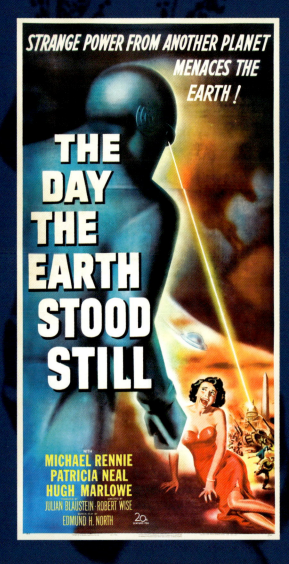

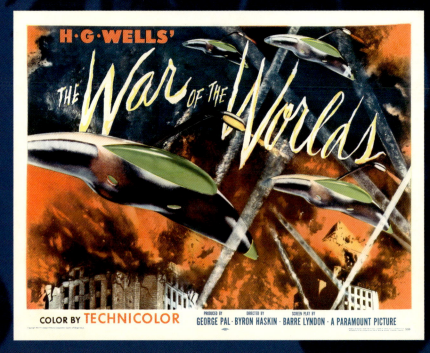

THE WAR OF THE WORLDS
Half-sheet, warning notice prop

This prop was actually used in the film as a description of the invading aliens and the Martian war machines they used to wreak havoc amongst us puny earthlings. The alien-to-human scale in the corner is great!

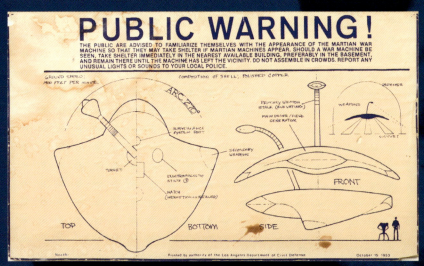

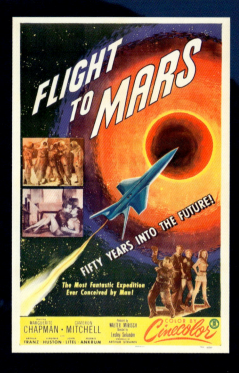

FLIGHT TO MARS *U.S. one-sheet*

WHEN WORLDS COLLIDE *Half-sheet*

Both these sci-fi movies have very cool
rocket ships that look more like today's jets
than they do spaceships.

INVADERS FROM MARS
Three-sheet, Martian suit prop

That was a big guy who was able to fit into
this suit from the film – it's huge! *Invaders
From Mars* is unique in that it is told from a
child's point of view – shot with vivid, pre-
psychedelic colors, stark camera angles, and
exaggerated characterizations throughout
the film... The hydrocephalic tentacled
alien leader is a favorite memory from my
childhood.

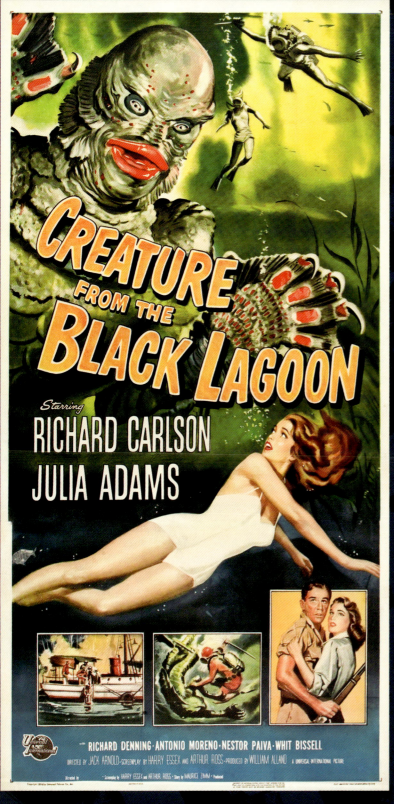

CREATURE FROM THE BLACK LAGOON   *Three-sheet, insert*

REVENGE OF THE CREATURE   *Insert, U.S. one-sheet, prop head*

CREATURE WALKS AMONG US   *U.S. one-sheet*

The Creature is considered one of the classic Universal horror monsters, and the only one that doesn't have a human origin, though he digs human women! The posters show the Creature in full terrorizing mode. *Revenge of the Creature* has the Creature terrorizing more females, and *Creature Walks Among Us* has the cool Golden Gate Bridge illustration, which is a personal favorite, being a San Francisco lad myself! The prop head to the right, from *Revenge of the Creature*, was sculpted by Bud Westmore.

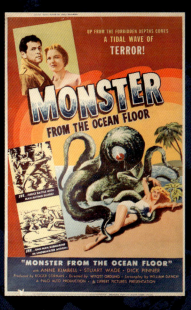

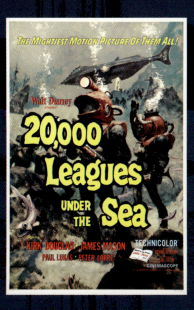

THIS ISLAND EARTH
One-sheet

One of the great sci-fi movies of its time. One of the aliens in this film, the Metaluna Mutant, is a very unusual, insectoidal, cool-looking creature.

IT CAME FROM BENEATH THE SEA   *Half-sheet*

MONSTER FROM THE OCEAN FLOOR
40" by 60" poster

GODZILLA   *One-sheet*

THE BEAST FROM 20,000 FATHOMS   *One-sheet*

These plots were driven by Cold War paranoia and the use of atomic weapons resulting in gigantic mutations spawned from the sea. *It Came from Beneath the Sea* was about an octopus that was awoken by atomic testing, as was *The Beast from 20,000 Fathoms*. *Godzilla* was the result of atomic bombing as was the giant amoeba from *Monster from the Ocean Floor*.

20,000 LEAGUES UNDER THE SEA   *One-sheet*

I love this adaptation of the Jules Verne classic and the cool underwater scene on the poster.

DAY THE WORLD ENDED *One-sheet*

TARANTULA *Half-sheet*

RODAN *40″ by 60″ poster*

THE BEAST WITH A MILLION EYES
Insert

Drive-in movie screens of the '50s — if it wasn't gigantic, it was from another world and/or radioactive! *Day the World Ended* has a great radiation-mutated monster designed by Paul Blaisdell. And *The Beast with a Million Eyes* clearly had only two, but the poster is intriguing!

FORBIDDEN PLANET *One-sheet, lobby card*

This film marks the debut of Robby the Robot, one of the most iconic robots this side of Gort!

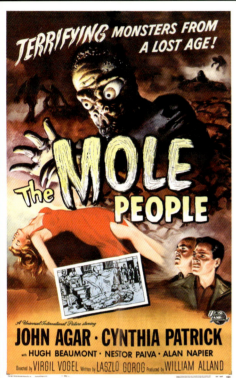

THE MOLE PEOPLE
U.S. one-sheet, half-sheet, prop head, and claw

The Mole People was about a subterranean race of albinos who lived in the hollow earth. The mutant albinos are the monsters shown here on the posters. Another Bud Westmore makeup job, the claw is a copy from the mold of the *Creature from the Black Lagoon* claw painted brown!

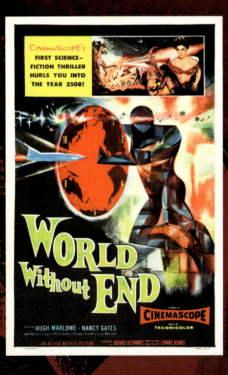

THE SHE CREATURE
U.S. one-sheet, half-sheet

C'mon, a monster with boobs and a bouffant? I love it! *The She Creature* is supercool! Monster designed by special effects master Paul Blaisdell.

WORLD WITHOUT END
U.S. one-sheet

Cool sci-fi graphic on this poster for a movie about time travel.

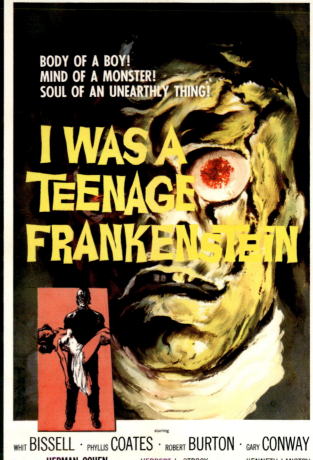

BODY OF A BOY!
MIND OF A MONSTER!
SOUL OF AN UNEARTHLY THING!

I WAS A TEENAGE FRANKENSTEIN

starring

WHIT **BISSELL** · PHYLLIS **COATES** · ROBERT **BURTON** · GARY **CONWAY**

Produced by **HERMAN COHEN** · Directed by **HERBERT L. STROCK** · Screenplay by **KENNETH LANGTRY**
A JAMES H. NICHOLSON-SAMUEL Z. ARKOFF PRODUCTION · **A METRO-GOLDWYN-MAYER RELEASE**

EVERY MAN ITS PRISONER...EVERY WOMAN ITS SLAVE!

IT CONQUERED THE WORLD

PETER GRAVES · BEVERLY GARLAND · LEE VAN CLEEF

**IT CONQUERED
THE WORLD**
*"It" prop,
half-sheet,
lobby card*

**I WAS A
TEENAGE
FRANKENSTEIN**
U.S. one-sheet

**I WAS A
TEENAGE
WEREWOLF**
U.S. one-sheet

That's not a monster, it's a legume! Thanks to
creative designer Paul Blaisdell, Beulah, the
monster from *It Conquered the World*, is one
of the most imaginative alien depictions in the
movies. No wonder it conquered the world! If
this saber-toothed cucumber-squash creature
came at me, I wouldn't have a chance! The
prop was the spawn of the Venusian alien used
in the film.

So what if the title is hokey, I really enjoyed
I Was a Teenage Frankenstein! The look of the
monster is really great. In fact I believe it was
the inspiration for the Shock Monster/Horror
Zombie image used so much in the '50s and
'60s. The last sequence of this film is in color!

I Was a Teenage Werewolf has a cool bucktoothed juvenile delinquent werewolf, and very
effective poster artwork!

The most amazing
motion picture
of our time!

I WAS A TEENAGE WEREWOLF

starring

MICHAEL **LANDON** · YVONNE **LIME** · WHIT **BISSELL** · TONY **MARSHALL**
Produced by **HERMAN COHEN** · Directed by **GENE FOWLER Jr.** · Screenplay by **RALPH THORNTON**
A JAMES NICHOLSON-SAMUEL Z. ARKOFF Production · **AN AMERICAN INTERNATIONAL PICTURE**

CURSE OF FRANKENSTEIN
British quad

This entry into the Frankenstein saga is the first in color, with Christopher Lee playing a horrifying monster.

INDESTRUCTIBLE MAN
U.S. one-sheet

This horror/sci-fi movie has a burlesque theater in the plot – better known as strip clubs these days, folks!

CURSE OF THE DEMON   *U.S. one-sheet*

Directed by Jacques Tourneur who also brought us *Cat People* and *I Walked with a Zombie*, this film was also called *Night of the Demon*. This is one of the first films to feature satanism in its plot. The main protagonist was loosely based on Aleister Crowley. The last part of the film, when you finally get to see the demon, is epic!

FROM HELL IT CAME   *U.S. one-sheet*

This is a hilarious-looking tree monster, courtesy of Paul Blaisdell. It's a great poster from a not so great film.

VOODOO WOMAN *Half-sheet*

One of the worst films in this book. So bad even I couldn't make time for it. The monster's costume is from *The She Creature*, though modified slightly.

DISEMBODIED *U.S. one-sheet*

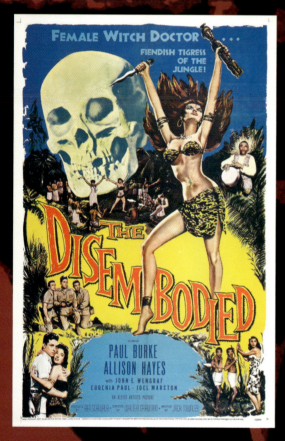

THE ASTOUNDING SHE MONSTER *One-sheet*

So astounding, her touch kills would-be suitors!

THE INVISIBLE BOY *Three-sheet*

Robby the Robot makes another appearance!

ZOMBIES OF MORA TAU *Half-sheet*

Underwater zombies guarding a shipwreck — brilliant!

BLOOD OF THE VAMPIRE *Half-sheet*

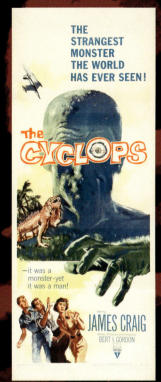

THE MONSTER THAT CHALLENGED
THE WORLD *U.S. one-sheet*

THE CYCLOPS *Insert*

THE BRAIN FROM PLANET AROUS *Half-sheet*

THE BLACK SCORPION *U.S. one-sheet*

THE 7TH VOYAGE OF SINBAD *Italian*

From giant slugs to giant brains to giant scorpions and a pair of Cyclops, these posters drive home the fact that anything unusually big is a horror!

I MARRIED A MONSTER FROM OUTER SPACE *U.S. one-sheet*

THE BRIDE AND THE BEAST *U.S. one-sheet*

What could be scarier than waking to find you are married to an alien or a beast! *I Married a Monster from Outer Space* has some chilling moments and a cool-looking alien.

THE AMAZING COLOSSAL MAN *U.S. one-sheet*

WAR OF THE COLOSSAL BEAST *Half-sheet*

The Colossal Man was another victim of atomic weaponry. In the sequel, he turns into the Colossal Beast after falling off Hoover Dam. I always wondered where his really large diaper came from.

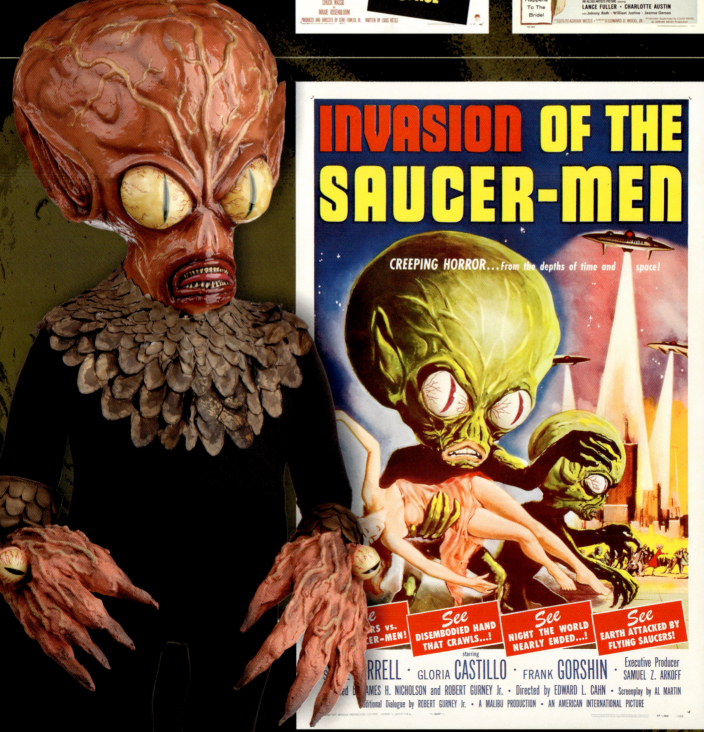

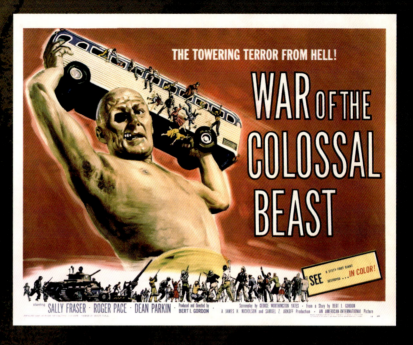

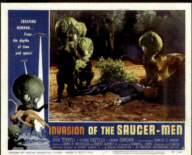

INVASION OF THE SAUCERMEN

U.S. one-sheet, British quad, four lobby cards. Saucerman figure re-creation. Saucerman collar prop. Saucerman weapon prop

One of my all-time fave '50s sci-fi movies, the plot is a bit innocent until the Saucermen land. Then it turns into a full-on invasion! The poster illustration is an accurate depiction of what the aliens look like in the movie, which wasn't always the case in the '50s! As a kid, I always wondered why aliens were so interested in our earth women!

The collar on this Saucerman recreation was one of the collars used in the film. The Saucerman head is made from a mold of one of the original Paul Blaisdell–designed heads.

WHO WILL
BE HIS
BRIDE
TONIGHT
?

HAMMER FILM PRODUCTIONS, LTD. PRESENTS

HORROR OF DRACULA

ALL NEW! in Brilliant TECHNICOLOR!

Starring PETER CUSHING also starring MICHAEL GOUGH and MELISSA STRIBLING with CHRISTOPHER LEE as DRACULA

Screenplay by JIMMY SANGSTER • From the novel by BRAM STOKER • Directed by TERENCE FISHER • Executive producer MICHAEL CARRERAS • Associate producer ANTHONY NELSON-KEYS • Produced by ANTHONY HINDS

A UNIVERSAL-INTERNATIONAL RELEASE

NEW AND GREATEST FRANKENSTEIN MONSTERPIECE!!

"THE REVENGE OF FRANKENSTEIN"

WE DARE YOU TO SEE IT!
WE DOUBLE-DARE YOU
TO FORGET IT!

If you go alone ...you'll find yourself running all the way home!

SUPER-NATURAL TECHNICOLOR

Starring PETER CUSHING • EUNICE GAYSON • FRANCIS MATTHEWS • MICHAEL GWYNN

Written by JIMMY SANGSTER • Produced by ANTHONY HINDS • Directed by TERENCE FISHER • A HAMMER FILM PRODUCTION • A COLUMBIA PICTURE

Universal Film, Inc.

LE CAUCHEMAR DE DRACULA

with PETER CUSHING • MICHAEL GOUGH • MELISSA STRIBLING et CHRISTOPHER LEE dans le rôle de DRACULA
Une Production HAMMER FILM EN COULEURS • Mise en scène TERENCE FISHER

INTERDIT AUX MOINS DE 16 ANS

HORROR OF DRACULA ALL NEW!

HORROR OF DRACULA ALL NEW!

HORROR OF DRACULA
U.S. one-sheet, French grande, two lobby cards

THE REVENGE OF FRANKENSTEIN   *U.S. one-sheet*

FRANKENSTEIN 1970   *U.S. one-sheet*

The Dracula film was made after the huge success of *The Curse Of Frankenstein*. Christopher Lee made a particularly effective Dracula, a role he would play for the next twenty years! He was also the first cinematic vampire shown with fangs drenched in the blood of his victims. And *The Curse of Frankenstein* was so popular, Hammer Studios felt compelled to make the first of many sequels in *The Revenge of Frankenstein*. On the other side of the pond, the effort to bring back Karloff to the Frankenstein opus was less successful in *Frankenstein 1970*. Why do these monsters always know where all the hot women are?

ALLIED ARTISTS presents

BORIS KARLOFF

"FRANKENSTEIN 1970"

WARNING!
"Frankenstein 1970" is the most blood-freezing horror ever created! This picture may be too dangerous for people with weak hearts! Beware!

FILMED IN CinemaScope

co-starring TOM DUGGAN • JANA LUND • DONALD BARRY • CHARLOTTE AUSTIN

Produced by AUBREY SCHENCK • Directed by HOWARD W. KOCH • Screenplay by RICHARD LANDAU and GEORGE WORTHINGTON YATES

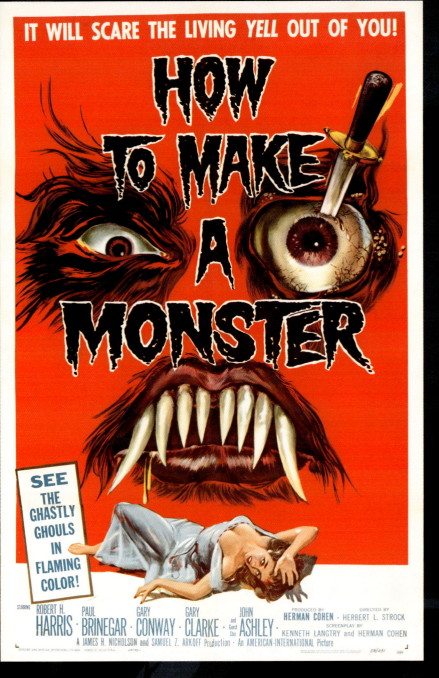

HOW TO MAKE A MONSTER
U.S. one-sheet

THE CRAWLING EYE *U.S. one-sheet*

FIEND WITHOUT A FACE *U.S. one-sheet*

It will scare the living yell out of you! Love that tag line! This movie was meant to be a follow-up to the *I Was a Teenage Frankenstein/Werewolf* movies, with a lot of the same actors and props recycled from those films. Great poster with a montage of the two monsters together and a knife in the eye to boot.

Faceless fiends and crawling eyes, sometimes the titles were way better than the movies themselves. *The Crawling Eye* poster is hilarious! *It! The Terror from Beyond Space* was the first movie with a stowaway alien on an earth-bound spaceship.

IT! THE TERROR FROM BEYOND SPACE
Half-sheet

CURSE OF THE FACELESS MAN/IT! THE TERROR FROM BEYOND SPACE
Double-bill combo poster

MACABRE *U.S. one-sheet*

THE UNDEAD *Insert*

SCREAMING SKULL *Insert*

The skulls have come for our women! These three posters have killer skull graphics. but the only real horror movie is *Screaming Skull. Macabre* is more of a Hitchcock-type thriller, while *The Undead* is a medieval period piece.

THE ANGRY RED PLANET *Half-sheet*

The Angry Red Planet has a cool Martian monster in the bat-spider-rat-crab, as seen on the poster.

THE SPIDER *U.S. one-sheet*

THE
MONSTER
OF PIEDRAS
BLANCAS
Insert

THE
ALLIGATOR
PEOPLE
U.S. one-sheet

NIGHT OF
THE BLOOD
BEAST
U.S. one-sheet

FRANK-
ENSTEIN'S
DAUGHTER
Half-sheet

Night of the Blood Beast is knocked for its bad script, but I think it's great! *The Monster of Piedras Blancas* is a great movie with a cool monster. Again, the costume is made of recycled parts from other monsters — the legs are from the Metaluna Mutant and the claws are from *The Creature from the Black Lagoon*. *Frankenstein's Daughter* is one of those movies that's so bad, it's good!

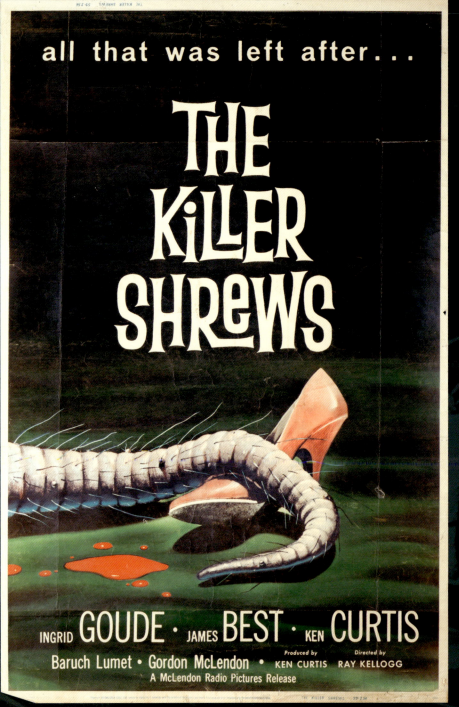

all that was left after...

THE KILLER SHREWS

INGRID GOUDE · JAMES BEST · KEN CURTIS

Baruch Lumet · Gordon McLendon · Produced by KEN CURTIS · Directed by RAY KELLOGG
A McLendon Radio Pictures Release

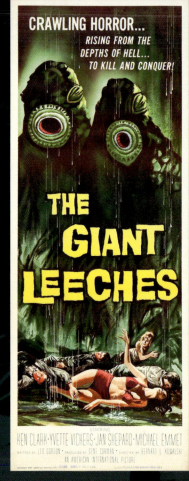

CRAWLING HORROR...
RISING FROM THE DEPTHS OF HELL... TO KILL AND CONQUER!

THE GIANT LEECHES

STARRING
KEN CLARK · YVETTE VICKERS · JAN SHEPARD · MICHAEL EMMET

WHEN THE SCREEN SCREAMS
YOU'LL SCREAM TOO...
IF YOU VALUE YOUR LIFE!

PERCEPTO!
newest and most startling gimmick on the screen!...

COLUMBIA PICTURES
The Tingler

GUARANTEED

starring VINCENT PRICE
with JUDITH EVELYN
DARRYL HICKMAN · PATRICIA CUTTS
A WILLIAM CASTLE PRODUCTION

THE KILLER SHREWS
U.S. one-sheet

THE GIANT LEECHES
Insert

**THE FOUR SKULLS
OF JONATHAN DRAKE**
Half-sheet

THE TINGLER
U.S. one-sheet

"THE FOUR SKULLS OF JONATHAN DRAKE"

Four Money NOT Returned If You Faint!

This Picture Was Written, Produced and Directed to SCARE THE DAYLIGHTS OUT OF YOU!

He was custodian of the icebox that kept the skulls crisp and fresh!

THE DOCTOR WHO IS ALWAYS COOKING UP SOME FRIGHTENING SKULLDUGGERY!

Featuring
EDUARD FRANZ
VALERIE FRENCH
GRANT RICHARDS · HENRY DANIELL

The Killer Shrews is one of those films that looks better than it is. *The Giant Leeches* is a better film than it looks! In *The Tingler*, Vincent Price's character experiments with LSD, the first reference to that drug on film. The bloody bathtub scene is shot in color while the rest of the film is in black-and-white! On *The Four Skulls of Jonathan Drake* poster is Zutai, the character with a stitched-up mouth. Unique and creepy!

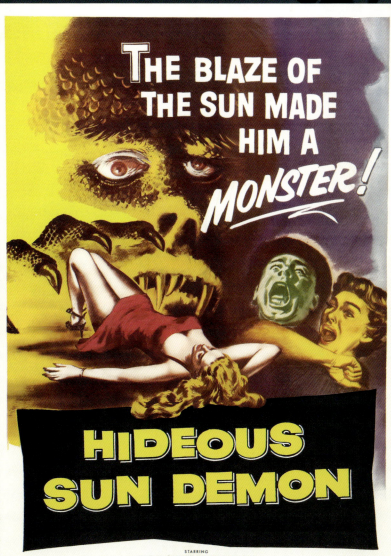

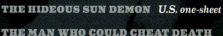

THE COLOSSUS OF NEW YORK *Half-sheet*

THE MUMMY *U.S. one-sheet*

THE HIDEOUS SUN DEMON *U.S. one-sheet*

THE MAN WHO COULD CHEAT DEATH
U.S. one-sheet

The Colossus of New York is about a man whose
brain is put inside a robot. Loved this movie
when I was a kid! *The Mummy* is a Hammer
Studios remake, very cool and moody. *The
Hideous Sun Demon* is another one of my favorite
monsters. I love the title and the concept of a
man turning into a monster in the sunlight!
I have not seen *The Man Who Could Cheat Death*
but I love the two-face image on this poster.

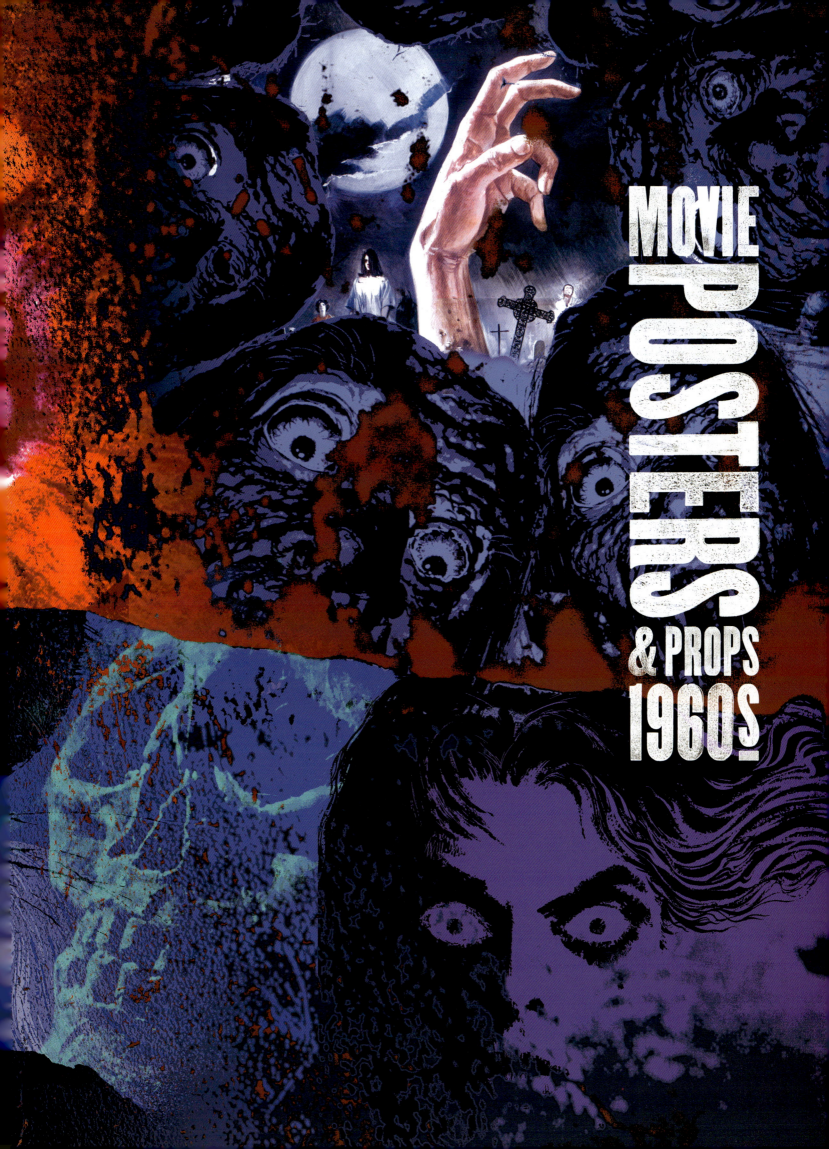

MOVIE POSTERS

& PROPS 1960s

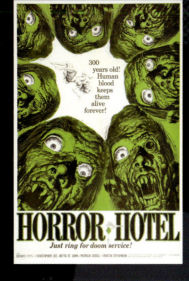

HORROR HOTEL
The designer of this great poster got a lot of mileage out of that one ghoul head!

BLACK SUNDAY
A highly influential masterpiece! Directed by Mario Bava, it's about a woman who discovers she is the reincarnation of an evil witch executed in an iron maiden.

PSYCHO
This Hitchcock masterpiece upped the ante for horror films, with its themes of graphic sex and violence. The shower scene is one of cinema's finest moments, in terms of sheer terror! *Psycho* spawned numerous copycat horror films, but has never been eclipsed.

MOTHRA
Mothra starts as a caterpillar, spins a huge cocoon on Tokyo Tower, then turns into a moth! The twin singing fairies could communicate with Mothra telepathically. More a fantasy film than a horror movie.

HORRORS OF SPIDER ISLAND
This was a lost film until just recently. I always thought the monster on the poster was cool.

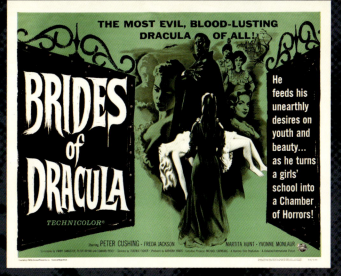

WHAT EVER
HAPPENED TO
BABY JANE?
A great
psychological
horror movie,
kind of like *Sunset
Blvd.* gone horribly
wrong. Bette Davis
is truly terrifying!

BRIDES
OF DRACULA
Blood. lust.
unearthly desires.
'Nuff said.

CARNIVAL OF SOULS
A truly nightmarish film that borders on
the surreal, this British poster captures the
haunted mood of the main character very
accurately.

GORGO
Poor Gorgo. all he wanted to do was to get
back to his mama ... who was about three
times as big as he! I really connected with
this movie when I was younger, and the
poster is exciting and action-packed!

BURN WITCH BURN
Really great font on the title. Based on
a story called *Conjure Wife,* also about
witches and a satanic cult, you know, all
the good stuff!

NIGHTMARE CASTLE
Barbara Steele as both ghost and victim.

TOMB OF LIGEIA
Great poster of an Edgar Allen Poe film adaptation.

THE INCREDIBLY STRANGE CREATURES WHO STOPPED LIVING AND BECAME MIXED-UP ZOMBIES

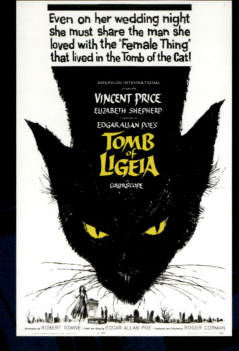

THE HORROR OF PARTY BEACH/ THE CURSE OF THE LIVING CORPSE
The Horror of Party Beach was a big hit with my friends and me in second grade — women in bikinis being attacked by radioactive creatures!

GHIDRAH THE THREE-HEADED MONSTER
This is the first appearance of Ghidrah, who was always my favorite Japanese monster. In this film there is a hilarious scene where Godzilla, Rodan, and Mothra have a three-way conversation about whether to join forces to defeat Ghidrah. Priceless!

PLANET OF THE VAMPIRES
Vampires from outer space! Not really, but this futuristic sci-fi vampire movie delivers on all fronts in my opinion. I think the film might have been an influence on Ridley Scott and the Alien series.

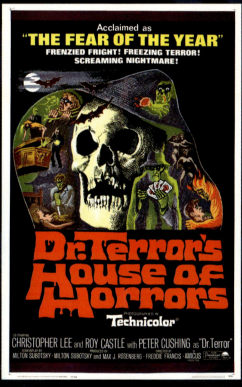

DIE, MONSTER, DIE!

Based on the Lovecraft story "The Color out of Space," this was a great vehicle for the aging Boris Karloff. The poster image of him is creepy!

TWO ON A GUILLOTINE

About the second or third horror movie I ever saw. Not much has been written about it, but it is a decent film about a crazy magician.

FRANKENSTEIN MEETS THE SPACE MONSTER/CURSE OF THE VOODOO

Cool battle scene between Frankenstein and a bizarre-looking space monster.

DR. TERROR'S HOUSE OF HORRORS

I have a soft spot for collage-like posters that show scenes from the film. This is one of the coolest! This film is actually five stories within a main story, with a good twist ending.

REPULSION

Roman Polanski does a fine job taking the viewer to the edge of insanity in this classic psychological horror film. The colors on this poster are twisted and fantastic!

THE EVIL OF FRANKENSTEIN

The makeup of the monster on this poster is similar to the original Frankenstein monster makeup.

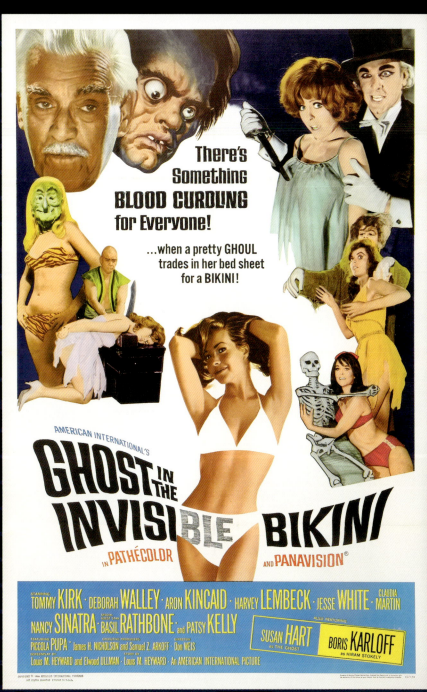

THE REPTILE
The monster's appearance in this movie was always very frightening to me. The head shot of her is perfect!

DRACULA PRINCE OF DARKNESS/ THE PLAGUE OF THE ZOMBIES
Great combo poster of two great Hammer films. Check out the gender-specific freebies you got when you entered the theater.

THE UNDERTAKER AND HIS PALS
This is one of the great posters of the early '60s. Girls undressing on a coffin? C'mon!

QUEEN OF BLOOD
Now here's a vampire from outer space, though you can't really tell from the poster. I thought the green-skinned Queen was superhot back then!

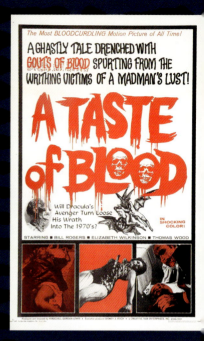

FANTASTIC VOYAGE
This Japanese poster is the best piece I've seen on this sci-fi classic, about a group of surgeons miniaturized and injected into a person's body to work on a blood clot in the brain. Brilliant stuff!

A TASTE OF BLOOD
Hilarious plot about a guy who drinks, then the booze turns him into a vampire!

FRANKENSTEIN CREATED WOMAN
One of my favorite Hammer films from the '60s, I remember seeing this one at the theater!

DESTROY ALL MONSTERS
Ultimate fighting, Toho style! This is when all the monsters fight Ghidrah, yet again! Check out how Godzilla, Mothra, Rodan, and Manda got star billing on this poster!

GHOST IN THE INVISIBLE BIKINI
Great title, this is a fun film if you were a little kid when you first saw it, as I was.

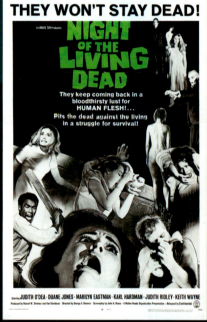

NIGHT OF THE LIVING DEAD
I still get creeped out when I watch this! The cemetery scene is great. The house sequence is great. Everything is great in this landmark zombie film! The British quad is good, but notice that there are no zombies on the poster!

ROSEMARY'S BABY
"He's got his father's eyes!" Yes, only problem is, his father is Satan! I think of this movie every time I hear someone say that about their children.

FRANKENSTEIN
MUST BE DESTROYED
There is a lot of head drilling in this film. Frankenstein's creation does not look as horrorific this time as it has in other Hammer horror films.

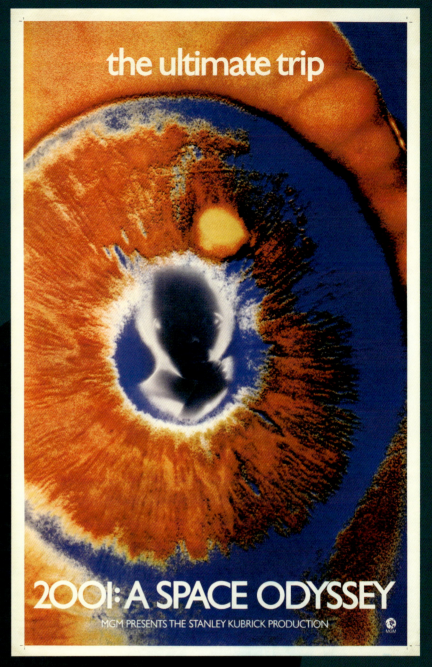

BARBARELLA
2001: A SPACE ODYSSEY
At age seven, I saw this film at the
Coronet Theater in San Francisco
with my father, and it blew my
mind! This poster is the rarest style
of the many one-sheets available.

THE GREEN SLIME
This film scared the living yell out
of me as a kid. When I saw it as an
adult, I laughed through most of it!

ASTRO ZOMBIES
"With one wave of my flaming
hand I send my Astro Zombies to
destroy your world." So says Glenn
Danzig in the Misfits song "Astro
Zombies." This poster has a great
image of the Astro Zombie wearing
a suit jacket while menacing a girl!

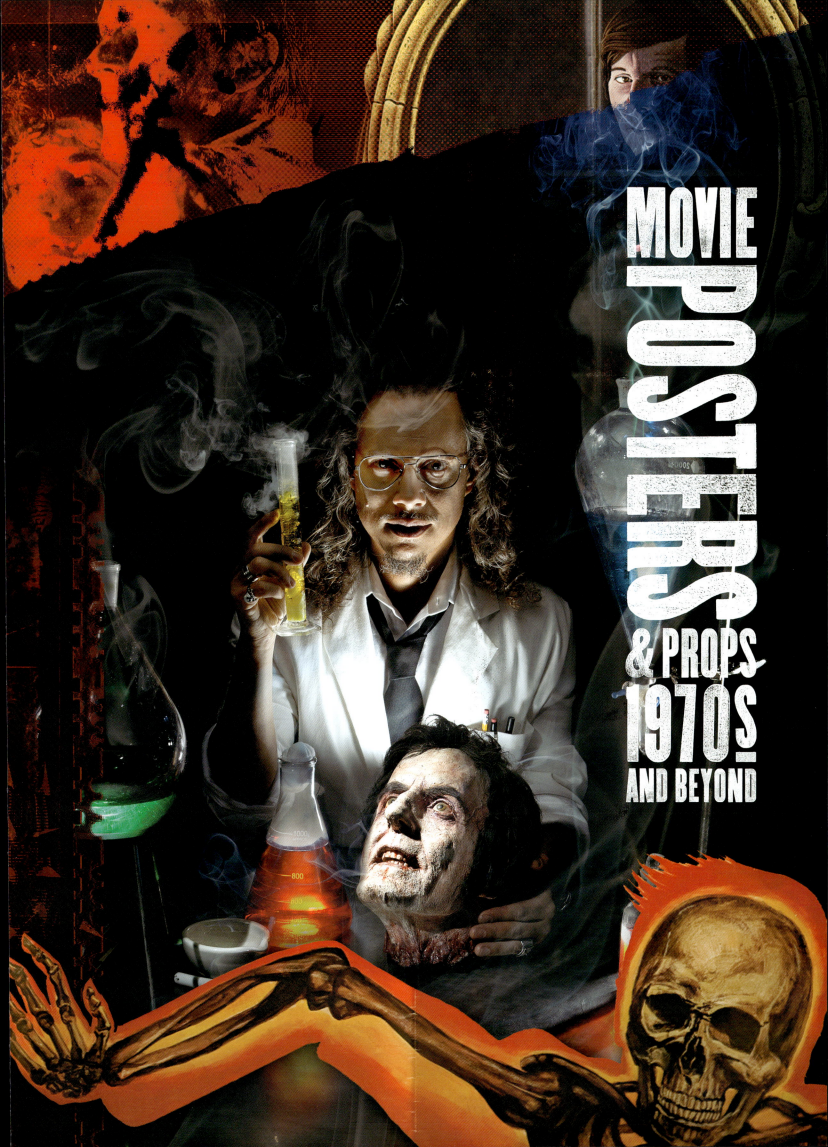

MOVIE POSTERS & PROPS 1970s AND BEYOND

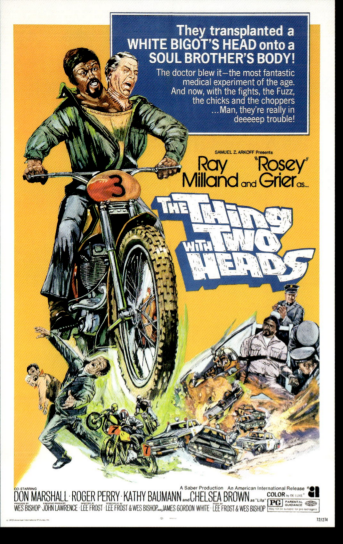

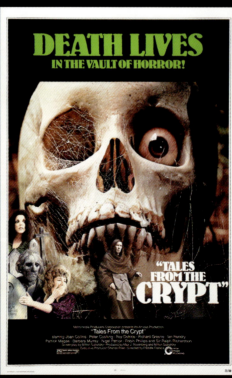

THE INCREDIBLE 2-HEADED TRANSPLANT

THE THING WITH TWO HEADS

Watch out for these two doubleheaders!
I thought this storyline was brilliant
as a kid. I saw this combo at the movie
theater. TWICE!

TALES FROM THE CRYPT

Of all the horror anthology movies that came out
back then, I enjoyed this one the most.

HOUSE OF DARK SHADOWS

The female vampire image on this poster
really jumps out and grabs your throat! I
think this is one of the few posters I've seen
with a staked-through-the-heart vampire.

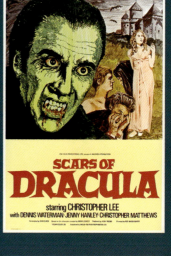

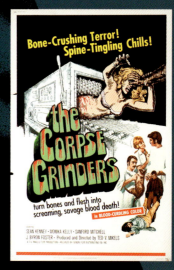

EQUINOX
One of my all-time favorite films. this Lovecraftian occult story is next level. It probably inspired Sam Raimi. to a certain point. to write the script to *The Evil Dead*. because there are a lot of similarities. The blue ape-demon on the poster was very unique. and for such a low-budget production. this movie looked great!

DRACULA VS. FRANKENSTEIN
Dracula with a perm? Kenneth Strickfaden. the electrical genius who did the lab effects for the original *Frankenstein. Bride of Frankenstein. Mask of Fu Manchu*. etc.. also did the lab effects in this movie. a real cult classic that I love to death! This was Lon Chaney. Jr.'s last horror film.

SCARS OF DRACULA
I like the big green Dracula face! The background looks like a medieval painting.

THE HOUSE THAT DRIPPED BLOOD
The skull/face juxtaposition on this poster is pure genius. Looks like a Pushead drawing.

THE CORPSE GRINDERS
The poster art reminds me of the cover art of the pre-code horror comic covers of the '50s! Totally demented visual. a classic!

The Count is back, with an eye for London's hotpants... and a taste for everything.

DRACULA A.D. 1972

A Hammer Production starring CHRISTOPHER LEE · PETER CUSHING And starring STEPHANIE BEACHAM CHRISTOPHER NEAME · MICHAEL COLES · Screenplay by DON HOUGHTON · Executive Producer MICHAEL CARRERAS · Produced by JOSEPHINE DOUGLAS Directed by ALAN GIBSON · from Warner Bros., a Warner Communications Company **PG**

And... for Lovers of the Macabre

WARNER BROS. presents A HAMMER FILM PRODUCTION

CRESCENDO

STEFANIE POWERS · JAMES OLSON · Margaretta SCOTT · Jane LaPOTAIRE · Joss ACKLAND Directed by ALAN GIBSON · Screenplay by JIMMY SANGSTER and ALFRED SHAUGHNESSY · Producer MICHAEL CARRERAS · Executive Producer ALAN GIBSON · TECHNICOLOR **PG**

72/394

BLOODSUCKER!

Deadlier than Dracula!

Warm young bodies will feed his hunger and hot, fresh blood his awful thirst!

"BLACULA' IS THE MOST HORRIFYING FILM OF THE DECADE." —Count Dracula Society

BLACULA

"BLACULA" STARRING WILLIAM MARSHALL · DENISE NICHOLAS · VONETTA McGEE **PG** GORDON PINSENT AND THALMUS RASULALA ALSO STARRING EMILY · LANCE · CHARLES · COLOR YANCY · TAYLOR, Sr. AND MACAULAY As DRACULA By DeLuxe PRODUCED BY JOSEPH T. NAAR DIRECTED BY WILLIAM CRAIN WRITTEN BY JOAN TORRES AND RAYMOND KOENIG MUSIC COMPOSED BY GENE PAGE · An American International Picture

72/250

BLACULA

IN THE YEAR 2000 HIT AND RUN DRIVING IS NO LONGER A FELONY. IT'S THE NATIONAL SPORT!

DAVID CARRADINE DEATH RACE 2000

DEATH RACE 2000 A CROSS COUNTRY ROAD WRECK

CO-STARRING SIMONE GRIFFETH · SYLVESTER STALLONE · LOUISA MORITZ · DON STEELE Screenplay by ROBERT THOM and CHARLES B. GRIFFITH · Original Story by IB MELCHIOR · Produced by ROGER CORMAN · Directed by PAUL BARTEL METROCOLOR **R** RESTRICTED

THE MOST HORRIFYING FILM YOU'LL EVER SEE IN YOUR LIFE!

NOTHING HAS EVER STRIPPED YOUR NERVES AS SCREAMINGLY RAW AS

THE GORE GORE GIRLS

STARRING
★ FRANK KRESS ★ AMY FARRELL
★ HEDDA LUBIN
★ HENNY YOUNGMAN

special effects by the same perverted madmen who brought you
BLOOD FEAST TWO THOUSAND MANIACS!
THE GRUESOME TWOSOME

IN SCREAMING COLOR

NOTICE. PERSONS WITH HEART CONDITIONS PROHIBITED FROM ENTERING THIS THEATRE.

WARNING No one under 17 will be admitted unless parents accept responsibility

PRODUCED & DIRECTED BY HERSCHELL GORDON LEWIS

RELEASED BY

THE GORE GORE GIRLS

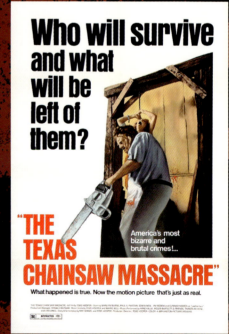

Who will survive and what will be left of them?

"THE TEXAS CHAINSAW MASSACRE"

America's most bizarre and brutal crimes!...

What happened is true. Now the motion picture that's just as real.

R RESTRICTED

DEATH RACE 2000
Great poster to this film. it's also a riot. with David Carradine as a race car driver named Frankenstein.

THE GORE GORE GIRLS
What a title! How can you not like a poster with a title like this?

THE TEXAS CHAINSAW MASSACRE
Much has been said about this landmark horror film. and deservedly so. Watching this movie when I was a kid gave me nightmares for months!

DRACULA A.D. 1972
Dracula comes back and parties his way through London! A Bay Area band called Stoneground was featured in this film.

BLACULA
BLOODSUCKER! This movie was huge among us kids when it came out. The poster shows a stake in his heart. Classic!

THE OMEN
Horror movies with Catholic themes, like *The Omen* and *The Exorcist*, gave me an opportunity to root for the bad guys (or demons!).

SOYLENT GREEN
"SOYLENT GREEN ARE PEOPLE!" screams Charlton Heston, once he found the truth about Soylent Green, a food substance in the film.

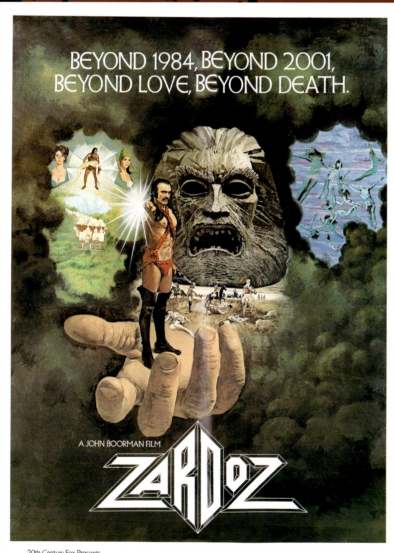

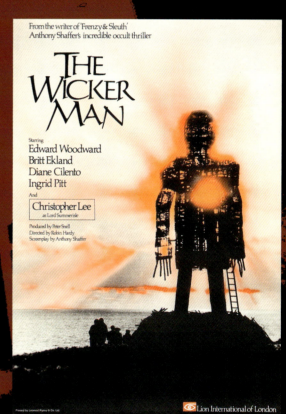

ZARDOZ
I like this film and I like this poster. Why? Because during the entire film, Sean Connery is wearing a suit that looks like he borrowed it from VAMPIRELLA!

THE WICKER MAN
Was this classic occult horror film the inspiration for the Burning Man event?

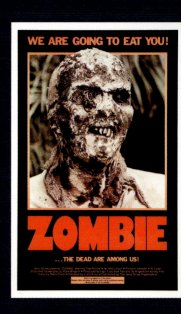

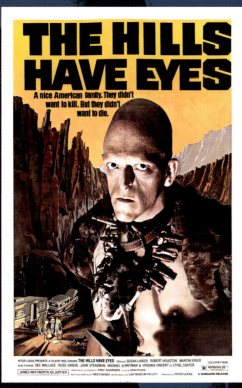

MAGIC
Let's face it — evil puppets, like evil clowns, are terrifying! The picture on the poster is cleverly cropped over the mouth of the puppet, which creates the question of who is the puppet, and who is the master.

THE HILLS HAVE EYES
"MMMMMM. BABY," says Pluto, the Michael Berryman character gracing the poster for this nice little vacation film.

CARRIE
This film adaptation of the novel was my first introduction to Stephen King, a true virtuoso of fright. The bloody shot of Carrie about to go medieval is iconic!

JAWS
A lot of people don't see this film as a horror movie, but I certainly do. I know people who stay out of the water to this day because they were so frightened by this flick.

ZOMBIE
Some of the coolest zombie scenes of the '70s were in this picture.

HALLOWEEN
Michael Myers is evil personified in this genre-defining slasher flick. This movie is very unsettling and filled with suspense and terror!

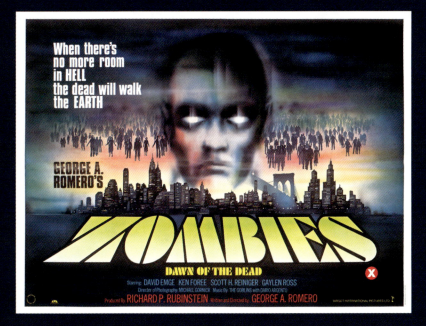

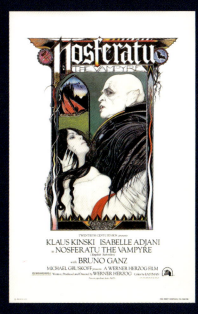

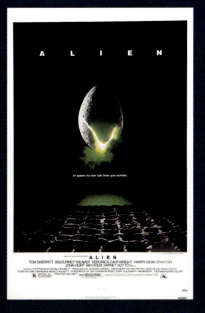

DAWN OF THE DEAD
"When there's no more room in hell the dead will walk the earth." Cliff Burton would always quote that line from this, one of his favorite movies. He would always sneak this flick into the videotape player on the tour bus, and I never minded watching it, time and again.

PHANTASM
Another '70s classic, with a creepy undertaker, flying silver spheres, and alien dwarves. Notice the red background is shaped like a tombstone.

NOSFERATU THE VAMPIRE
Klaus Kinski brought a certain degree of madness to his portrayal of Nosferatu. This film is bleak and foreboding, like any artful vampire movie should be. The artwork on this poster is first rate, more goth than the original movie's expressionistic poster.

RABID
Brilliant sci-fi horror film by David Cronenberg, starring a fully clothed Marilyn Chambers.

ALIEN
What can I say that has not been already said about this sci-fi horror classic? The iconic H. R. Giger–designed monster was one of the coolest creatures to come down the horror highway since the Creature from the Black Lagoon. The film had award-winning special effects, and the chestburster scene was truly startling!

**They were warned… They are doomed…
And on Friday the 13th, nothing will save them.**

FRIDAY THE THIRTEENTH

Obviously inspired by *Halloween*, this was the start of the saga that ran for twelve films. Jason isn't really in the plot of this movie, the writers brought him back from the dead for the sequels, and he didn't find a hockey mask until the third film. The props shown here were used in *Jason Goes to Hell*.

SCANNERS

Who wouldn't want to see a film whose plot revolved around exploding heads? The makeup was done by Dick Smith, who worked on *The Exorcist*.

THE HOWLING

Great modern revision of the werewolf legend, with outstanding special effects. I LOVE the scene when the werewolf, Eddie, says "Let me give you a piece of my mind," and then proceeds to do just that!

The tide of terror that swept America IS HERE

FROM BEYOND
A film adaptation loosely based on an H. P. Lovecraft short story, this totally psychotic film, about creatures and mutated beings from another dimension, is one of the best horror films of the '80s, in my opinion.

THE SHINING
Here's Johnny! Stanley Kubrick's other masterpiece does not resemble the book at all, but that is completely forgivable! His brilliantly imagined Overlook Hotel, with all its twisted, haunted guests, was very convincing. Credit goes to Stephen King for giving us the term "redrum."

AN AMERICAN WEREWOLF IN LONDON
I enjoy it when I see a good horror flick that has comedic elements. This movie has the right balance between screams and laughs, which along with the great Rick Baker effects, makes this a favorite of mine!

THE EVIL DEAD
EPIC occult horror film that depicts a man fighting his demons, literally, in a cabin in the middle of nowhere!

A NIGHTMARE ON ELM STREET

Wes Craven's idea of turning a good night's sleep into a killing realm for Freddy Krueger's victims is pure genius. The overhead perspective in this poster is great. The original film is still the best one as far as I'm concerned.

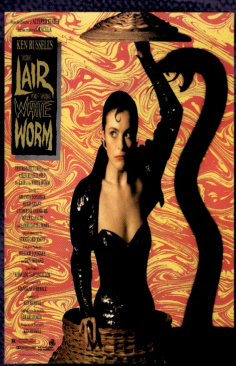

RE-ANIMATOR/THE FUNHOUSE/PRINCE OF DARKNESS

He was ahead of his time! One of my top ten horror movies of all time, *Re-Animator*'s plot is just too funny on paper, with mad doctors, zombie cats, and disembodied corpses. It has to be seen to be fully appreciated. H. P. Lovecraft would have loved this revision of his story! In *The Funhouse*, a Tobe Hooper film, the deformed son of the Funhouse owner parades around with a Frankenstein mask on. Very amusing! The final segment of John Carpenter's *Prince of Darkness* really creeped me out!

THE LAIR OF THE WHITE WORM

Loosely based on a story by Bram Stoker, this film is highly entertaining, the poster is visually striking, and Amanda Donohoe with the silhouette of the white worm looks fantastic!

HELLRAISER

S&M demons from another dimension!
Clive Barker's film is a masterpiece
of modern horror. Pinhead, the
leader of the Cenobites, is a carnal
being from another dimension who
has been described as both an angel
and a demon. The poster features a
stunning portrait of the Cenobite in all
his gory glory! Pinhead makeup from
Hellraiser: Hell on Earth.

EVIL DEAD 2

Ash still can't shake these demons in
this demonic comedy. The battle with
his possessed hand is over the top, and
the chainsaw as a body implement for
fighting demons is brilliant.

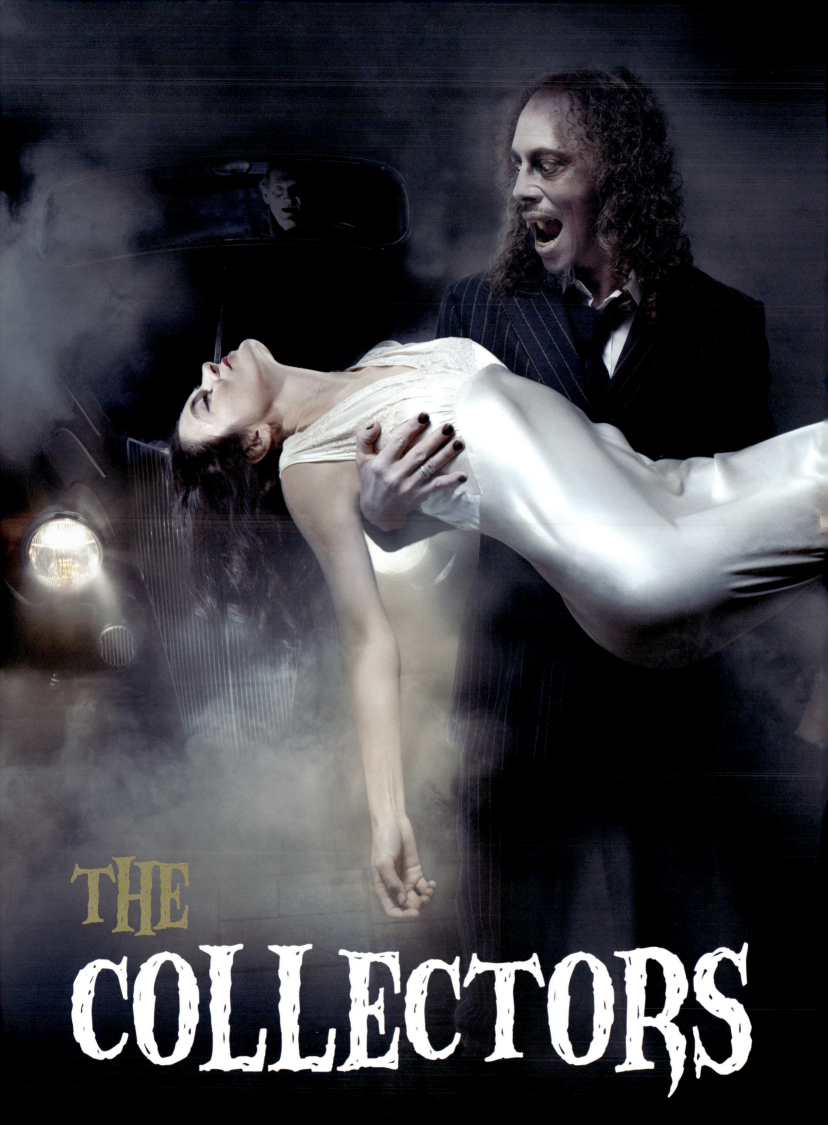

THE
COLLECTORS

A conversation with Kirk Hammett

PART 2

The whole nature of collecting is one that requires a specific mind-set and dedication. Many of us think that we collect things, but when juxtaposed alongside true collectors, we soon realize that we are no more than casual interlopers, compared to the obsessive enthusiasm and dedication of a true collector. Obviously, Kirk Hammett has earned the sort of capital that allows him to trade at the very highest tables of the collecting world. However, his core nature and reasons for collecting remain exactly the same as when he was a young boy. It is this that we discussed at length one afternoon, during a photo shoot at Kirk's San Francisco home. His friend Ron Moore, another passionate, famous collector on the scene, happened to be around on the same day, thus he spontaneously became part of the conversation.

SC So let's start this specific conversation with your take on the nature of collecting now versus the nature of collecting when you were a child. What are the differences? Is it essentially the same being?

KH When I collected back then it was very, very pure, very, very innocent, and it was driven exclusively by my love of these stories, these characters, the atmosphere, the visuals, the pure fantasy aspect of it all.... I was totally overtaken by this world that I wanted to exist in. So back then when I collected, the whole purpose was to fill my living space with this stuff, and then my mind could jump into some sort of fantasy land where I coexisted with all these characters in these strange situations and places. Now, my collecting motivations are virtually the same, except I also collect for rarity and for sentimental purposes, too. Take *The Invisible Man*. I first saw that great movie when I was a kid, and so today, staring at *The Invisible Man* poster will bring me to that moment in time when I was nine years old and spent a week walking around with bandages on my hands and face, pretending I was Claude Rains.

SC So some of today's collecting zeal is just pure sentimentality?

KH Yeah, for sure. And another part is because some of this stuff has yet to be seen. I never saw most of these posters when I was a kid because they hadn't been found. They weren't located. They were just hiding somewhere, available somewhere, maybe only in private collections, and many of them didn't surface for more than two decades. And there are all these weird stories about how these things were located. So the search becomes a sport because the hunt is so twisty. That spurs a determination to find it, and once you finally do acquire it and put it into the collection, that feeling is just the greatest in the world. And when you discover something like a *Frankenstein* one-sheet, it's a combination of a very successful treasure hunt and Christmas! You can't believe this thing of beauty has survived all these years. And you realize that you've just uncovered a historic piece of the pantheon of twentieth-century movie culture.

SC Let's discuss when you fell back into collecting, because obviously for the first few years of Metallica, you would have given the band everything.

KH Yeah, Metallica totally took over my life. I lived and breathed music, and when I took a break from all of that, it was to watch monster movies. So it was still on the periphery but music was my main thing. And then when I first heard Black Sabbath, I thought to myself, "Oh my God, these guys have it nailed on the head," because they were singing about all the stuff that I knew dearly—you know, the dark side and monsters and whatnot. And they're

named after a freaking horror movie from the '60s, and a lot of the imagery just naturally clicked with me.

SC So at some point you embarked back upon this earlier obsession.

KH In 1983 or '84 we were on tour, and I saw some *Famous Monsters* magazines in Canada, I think. They were on the newsstand like they were brand new, but they were actually shrink-wrapped, and I recognized them as being vintage. So I bought a bunch. And after that I started back in with posters that were more accessible from specialty stores that sold nothing but movie-related material. It was also around that time that I decided to start collecting toys again. In the back of *Famous Monsters* there were ads from the Captain Company that sold a lot of toys I couldn't afford when I was a kid, but a friend said he knew a guy whose sole job was finding vintage plastic models and reselling 'em. He said that he had all the old monster models, as well as car models, planes, and figure kits, so I called him up and started buying the monster ones. Then I met this other guy in the Midwest who was a toy dealer, and I'd ask him what he had from the '60s and '70s, and if he didn't have something, he knew other collectors who would. And that pretty much set me on my way. I started meeting other dealers and collectors, plus when I went on tour I started finding stuff in the various cities we hit. In a short amount of time I found I'd rediscovered the thread of collecting that I keep with me to this day for movie posters, monster toys, artwork, comics, books.

SC Obviously there's a lot more money coming into your life at this point. It's very clear the advantages that money can bring, but what are the disadvantages?

KH That would be "celebrity tax." Even during the time of *Ride the Lightning*, *Master of Puppets*, when Metallica didn't have the type of celebrity it has now, I realized that if I were talking to a certain dealer, there was a certain amount of celebrity tax being grafted onto everything just because of the fact that it was me they were dealing with.

SC And for the record, could we specify what "celebrity tax" is?

KH Extra money above what would be reasonable for the item in question. Someone will just conclude that I can afford another $50 on a $100 item. So what they would sell to person A for 100 bucks, they would sell to me for 150 bucks; the extra 50 being "celebrity tax." It happens on all levels.

So since early on, when I realized that this was going on, I've had people buy for me, which was a bit of a problem until I actually found someone I could trust. And Ron Moore is a fine example. Ron does almost all my movie poster transactions, and with posters it's really, really

The beginning of a
collection, circa 1987! I
could fit almost my entire
collection into this one shot.

tricky because we're potentially talking about thousands of dollars difference.

SC So Ron is essentially your agent in such matters?

KH Yeah. And he is very fair. We both make sure that what we're doing is always on the level because at the end of the day our reputations are at stake.... In this world, your word is everything.

SC OK, so explain to me a little more about the collecting world from the perspective of reputation. What, for example, would be a golden rule for all collectors?

KH Well, you never tell someone else what another collector has. If a collector invites you into their house to see his personal collection, you don't tell anyone what you've seen. If you don't know that rule, you don't get access to those coveted halls that hold these cherished objects. It's like a club, a secret society. And the reason is very logical. I'll explain. Say I have a *Dracula* insert, they have a *Frankenstein* insert, and the word is out that this *Frankenstein* insert's for sale. You say to this person, "I'll give you x amount of money for the *Frankenstein* insert," but this guy knows that you have a *Dracula* insert and he really wants that. So he'll say it isn't for sale, which forces you to ask why and explain that the word on the street is that it's for sale. And that person might then ask for the *Dracula* insert they know you have because someone told them. And then you have to tell them very politely that it's off the table. Just totally off the table. And depending on your relationship with them, and the type of person they are, either the deal goes through at that point or the deal falls flat. And yes, just because someone knows you have a *Dracula* poster they want, the initial *Frankenstein* deal could be off.

SC Is making a deal exciting? Let's say you want a certain item and there is this cat-and-mouse exchange over it. Is that exciting or is it just a drag?

KH It's exciting until you potentially blow the deal for whatever reason. Because when you blow the deal, you think you might not get another chance ever again in this lifetime. I've blown numerous deals just out of pure carelessness.

SC What do you mean?

KH Well, someone called me up one day and said, "I have some posters." And I barked at the guy that I wasn't buying posters. The guy said, "Even if it's a *Frankenstein* six-sheet?" I thought he was just exaggerating. So I said, "Yeah, I don't care if it's a *Frankenstein* six-sheet, I'm not buying posters right now. I can't afford it." Three or four days later, I hear someone bought a *Frankenstein* six-sheet. That was probably my worst mistake.

SC Do you know who bought it?

KH Oh yeah, of course I do. He's never gonna sell it, and I'm not even interested in approaching him on any sort of deal because he's probably gonna want the continent of Australia for it!

SC Would you say your collection is the best out there?

KH I see my collection as being maybe number two. The guy who has the number one collection in the world has just been doing it for the longest time. And you know, he was pretty much the first guy out of the gates when it comes to collecting this stuff, some thirty- or forty-odd years ago. There's another guy that has as good a collection as I do, and it's the same thing; he was one of the pioneers of movie memorabilia collecting and just got all the stuff before anyone else got into it. Those two guys cleaned up. When I came onto the scene, one thing I realized was that it really doesn't matter how much money you have, it's what you have to trade and who you know.

SC So they're not necessarily interested in the value of their collection, they are solely invested in what it is?

KH Every serious collector of this stuff really doesn't give a damn about the money. I know guys who have mortgaged their house a second time just to buy a one-sheet. I know guys who would sell out their mother for a deal or even for a rumor that there's a deal to be made somewhere.

SC So it's a form of addiction, then.

KH Yeah, and it's very cutthroat, too.

SC It sounds like gambling, Vegas-style.

KH It is. Recently, one individual went so far as to try to counterfeit this stuff. Of course he got caught, by the FBI of all people, and it brought the FBI into the whole world of movie poster collecting. So I recently got a phone call from the auction house saying, "Uh, your *Son of Frankenstein* window card is believed to be counterfeit." And I'm getting this call from the auction house because the auction house guy got a phone call from the FBI.

SC And what happens in that situation? They have to compensate you?

KH Yeah, of course. What happens is that I have to send the piece back to the auction house that I got it from. Then they have to get a forensic analysis of the poster paper.... Wait, my friend Ron can explain it even better. [Shouts outside to Ron] "Hey, Ron, could you come here for a minute please?"

[At this point, Ron Moore joins the conversation. —SC]

These are some mighty big fish!
Ron Moore and I with some cool
posters you might recognize!

Ron Moore Yeah, because these posters, these old [Venitrons] were all done on a French stone lithograph plate. And now these ink-jet prints are so high quality that they literally have to test the paper. And under an extreme magnification you can tell the difference between an original French stone lithography print and an ink-jet print. Because technology's come so far that they can reproduce these things to almost perfection. Yeah ... it will fool the naked eye.

SC Is part of the thrill of possessing an original vintage piece that you get to ponder the life it's had, who's owned it, and the history it carries?

KH Oh yeah. Some of these posters have very interesting stories. When *Nosferatu* came out in 1922 it was obviously a rip-off of *Dracula*, and Bram Stoker's widow sued the movie company and director. She won, and as a result of that lawsuit, all the prints of *Nosferatu*, all the movie posters—everything and anything that had to do with *Nosferatu*—was supposed to be destroyed, by court order. And as a result of that there's hardly anything on that movie available. The only reason I have that poster is because it's a Spanish issue that was sent to Spain before the court order to destroy everything was made. There are only three or four other pieces like it. This one was found in Barcelona.

SC So these rarities could be anywhere, and you have to be both prepared and ready to act fast to get them?

KH Oh yeah. Let me tell you a really crazy story, and this directly involves Ron. He called me up one day in the late '90s, and said that he'd found someone with six half-sheets. Both styles of the half-sheet on *Bride of Frankenstein*, *Dracula's Daughter*, *The Raven*, and *The Invisible Ray*. So a total of eight Universal horror half-sheets. One of those would have been an amazing find. Eight of them was jaw-dropping and just not heard of.

It'd be like the same person winning the lottery three times in a row.

RM So the guy sent me some photographs by e-mail, and even though they were kind of fuzzy, they looked legit.

SC Where was this guy?

RM In Wellington, New Zealand. He strictly wanted an offer because he had already called several auction houses—Christie's in South Kensington, Bonhams, several of them. So I called Kirk and told him what the guy had. Funny thing is, he had originally listed them in the equivalent of a small local paper's classifieds for $25 each, before he slowly started to learn what he had.

SC So where had this guy got the half-sheets from?

RM He remodeled homes for a living, and he had gone into a house where it would appear that the person who had lived there had worked for the Universal Poster Exchange—which was a distribution center for all the movie film prints, posters, and related materials, in the '30s—because they found everything in the attic, where they had thrown them on the floor to use as insulation.

SC Sorry? They were using stuff like this as insulation?

RM Yes. You know, paper is a great natural insulator. Before the days of the Dow Corning fiber, they used paper. So he found all these posters, all half-sheets, all U.S. paper, all Universal, from 1935 to 1936.

SC Did he get close to selling any for $25?

RM He got one response from someone who showed up at his house and said, "I'll take everything you've got." That spooked him. So he said that nothing was for sale anymore. He ended up going online and found out the posters were worth money, but because he couldn't find any for sale, he didn't realize how rare what he had was. His next step was calling Christie's–South Kensington and Bonhams, both in London. They started making him all sorts of wild predictions, like a half million dollars for the *Bride of Frankenstein* alone. And that didn't sound right to him either. So eventually, through word of mouth, he found me, called me, and I said, "Yeah, I'm real interested!" When I saw the pictures I said they looked legit. But are they in good shape? I remember he did not want to go through an auction house, he wanted to make a deal between us and leave it there.

I called Kirk: "What do you want to do?" And we worked out what it would retail for, a very realistic retail price. And we made the guy the offer, to which he said yes. I'm glad I had my passport in order, because I was off to Auckland, New Zealand, where I met the guy and got the posters. When he took 'em out of a tube and unrolled 'em in front of me, my jaw dropped. I had to put my best poker face on because I didn't know if these were gonna be legit or what shape they were in. We unrolled 'em, and they were the freshest colors I've ever seen on a poster. I mean, it was like very-fine to near-mint condition, all of 'em. They were just amazing. We call it "The New Zealand Find." Yeah.

SC How many of these did you buy? All of them, right?

RM Well, Kirk got one of each of the eight different pieces that were found. Then about two years later the people got back in touch with me and said, "We have more." My jaw dropped yet again. I would speculate that they'd always had them, but when I first met them they'd been very tight-lipped. They were very frightened, almost paranoid

of what they had. After I negotiated the deal for everything else in the second batch, all of a sudden they were very talkative!

KH Well, you know that ... I just wanted to say, that's not the only incident of someone tearing down or tearing apart walls or houses and finding movie posters in the walls. It's a fairly common occurrence. But it's always a crapshoot, you can never be sure of what you have. It's one in a million, like a needle in the haystack.

SC So taking that angle, have you ever researched Universal Studios employees from that era and tried to make contact with them?

KH We go through numerous scenarios. We strategize.

RM This is one of my favorite things to do. I have been all over this country looking for posters.

KH There was this one rare, super-rare piece. I wish I had it. A *Mask of Fu Manchu* insert, and it was pulled out of an old movie theater.

RM An old movie theater they were renovating, and it was underneath the carpet. It was being used to shim up the carpet. So over the years people had spilled Cokes and whatever, which had soaked through the carpet, and this thing was stained, nasty. But it actually restored pretty nicely. It looks beautiful now.

SC What would it cost to restore a poster of that nature?

RM One that bad, with all the staining in it? Could end up costing you $600 to restore it. But it's the only copy in existence.

SC That's pretty good. I was thinking thousands.

RM No, I think the most I've ever had to pay for the restoration of a piece was around $1,200, but for Kirk?

KH The French double-panel of *Frankenstein*, or the *Dracula's Daughter* six-sheet? They were a fortune, because the paper on those is so thick.

SC It sounds like mining for gold.

KH Funnily, I was saying to Ron recently that this sort of stuff brings out a form of "gold fever."

People get greedy. They think that they're looking at million-dollar pieces of paper when they're only like

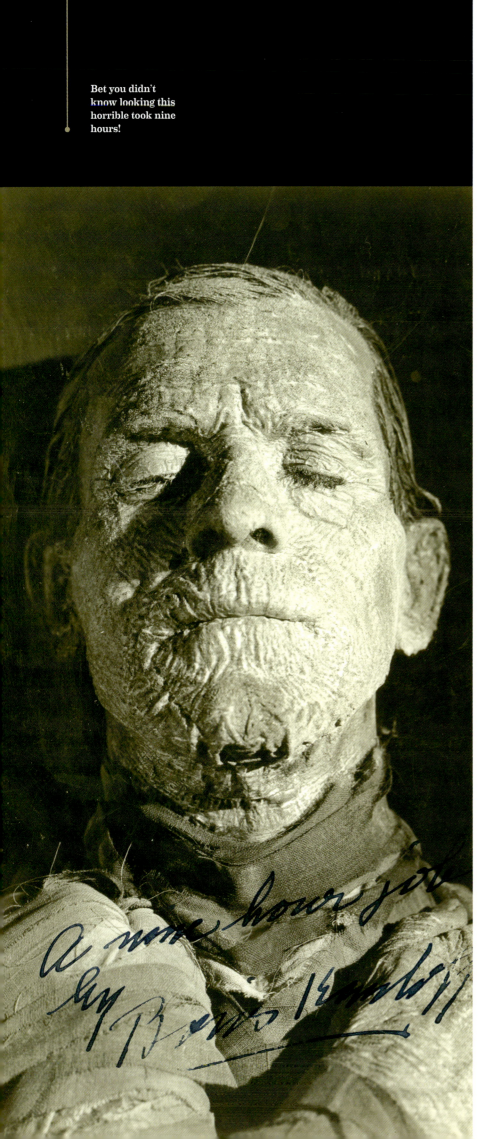

A nine hour job

Guy Bews [Ehrlof]

maybe a hundred dollars? It brings out a really bad quality in a person if that person does not know what they're looking at. The greed factor rises to the surface very quickly.

SC Looking at collecting from another angle, I remember when I accompanied you on a toy buy and the owner wouldn't let me into the house, only you....

KH I begged and pleaded. But at least the owner's wife brought out some cookies for you!

SC Indeed she did, but cookies aside, that seemed a little insane.

KH If it's any consolation, they wouldn't let me leave the kitchen.

SC You were telling me about that. They said you had to sit in a certain seat at a certain angle to the doorway, that way you didn't have a clear view of him coming in and out with the stuff.

RM I've known a few people like that. One of my favorite ones is when I was tracking down—and I've still never gotten to the bottom of it—an original U.S. one-sheet for *Metropolis*. And it's technically not known to exist because no one's seen it. But I did track down a guy who supposedly had it because I found the guy who said he sold it to him. I could not get him on the phone, and couldn't get to him any other way except to physically go there. So I went to his house, knocked on his door, and I had to have the conversation with him with the door "this" [gestures a narrow one-foot gap] far open.

SC That's fantastic.

RM And he would never admit to actually having it.

SC Was it a normal house? Did he have security gates?

RM No, it was actually very small, very plain. Old house.

KH You're also dealing with people who are pretty sober about these things. They're pretty even-keeled and sensible. But then you meet certain individuals and you instantly know they've never had a relationship with a male or a female ever before in their life, and you know that they've probably always stayed in a three-mile radius of their house. But they know these movies, they have these posters, and that's their life. And these are the people who aren't collectors. They just had this stuff since they were kids.

SC Have you ever managed through empathy to gain someone's trust enough to let you have a piece that they otherwise wouldn't have sold?

KH (looks at Ron Moore) You should tell him those stories.

RM (sighs) Kirk paid me very fair prices for pieces out of my collection. But I had no intention selling to anyone else ever. If they weren't for him, and I know he's got a love for it, and the fact that he also lets me have visitation rights, then I would never have sold.

SC Visitation rights. Ron, your use of language here is very telling. That's how it is, right?

KH (to Ron Moore) Well, tell him the story about that guy.

RM So there is *The Mummy* one-sheet. This is the only copy of the one-sheet known to exist.*

KH My mummy guitar is based on that poster right there. So that poster is familiar to most Metallica fans.

RM Here's how we got it, and I'll try to make it a somewhat concise story, but it's got so many details. I was sitting on the floor of my apartment one day and got a phone call from a guy who was asking, "So, you buy these movie posters. I got your name and number."
"Sure."
"What are you buying?"
So I went down the list: "Oh, sci-fi, Veronica Lake, Three Stooges, Humphrey Bogart," all these different areas I buy in, and I said of course the old Universal horror. And he goes, "Oh, you mean like those old Bela Lugosi, Boris Karloff things." I went, "Yeah, exactly," and he goes, "Yeah, I don't have any of those." And he says, "But, when I was in high school back in the early '60s, I knew this guy who had one in his bedroom." And then he says, "You know, I'll never forget it. It was just beautiful. It was Boris Karloff in *The Mummy*." And in my head I'm thinking, "Beautiful? Really? OK, I guess it's that Real Art reissue from 1951." And he's saying, "God, it had the greatest color." And I'm sitting there going, OK, that sounds pretty cool but no big deal. It was around 1993 when I got this call, and I thought it was this reissue, which was maybe worth $500. And then he goes, "Right next to Karloff it said IT COMES TO LIFE." Well, the phone almost fell out of my hand....

---

* See page 35 for a photo of this poster.

KH Because IT COMES TO LIFE is not on the reissue. It's only on the original issue.

RM So when he said that, I was thinking, "Oh my God, somebody who's got an original from '32?" So I said, "Do you think your buddy still has that?" And he said, "Oh, I'm sure he does, he's a pack rat. He never gets rid of anything."

KH God bless the pack rats.

RM So obviously I said I'd love to call him and see if he'd like to do anything with it. But it turned out that this guy had got into a huge falling out with the [pack rat] poster owner, and that he could only talk to this guy's parents! So it took me a month before he would tell me who the parents were, and from there I got the son's name and where he was. To which the guy said, "You can't tell him that you got his number from me. He'll hang up on you." He sounded very paranoid.

KH That's the thing; all these people are paranoid. And it's contagious, because I'm paranoid about it and I never used to be until I started collecting this stuff!

RM So I called the [pack rat] guy up with a cover story, and sure enough, when I called him he was like, "And how'd you get my name? How'd you hear about this poster?" He was very straightforward, very factual. And I just had to play along. Eventually I said, "Look, you know, God, I'd love to come see that poster. Do you still have it?" He goes, "Yes, it's hanging in my living room."
"I'd love to come see it."
"Well, you can. You know what? You can come over the next time I have movie night here at the house."
"Great, when's that?"
"Well, it's about a year from now. I only do it once a year and we just had it."
And I'm thinking, "Oh, my God."

KH Who has a movie night once a year?

RM Well, apparently he works a lot, he's an accountant, and just doesn't have time for it. So anyway, I had to say, "A year? I'm gonna have to wait a year?" I couldn't wait a year.

KH In the meantime, Ron called me up and told me it'd be a year. I said, *"No way am I gonna wait here for that poster to get bought by someone else, for a whole year!"*

RM So I'm trying everything I could....

KH And I'm screaming and yelling....

SC Were you really? Actually screaming?

KH Literally screaming and yelling.

RM I'm trying to figure out how am I gonna get to this guy. So I just kept calling. You know you run the risk of pissing somebody off, but I just kept calling. And I finally

While getting the
content together for
this book, April 2011.

got to the point after about two or three months where I would call once a week. He almost wouldn't even take my calls. About three or four months after the first contact, I was driving around L.A. one day, really close to his neighborhood, and I thought, "What the hell, I'll just call." And I said, "Hey, I'm only a few blocks away from you." I was being pretty flippant really because I figured the guy was simply going to tell me I couldn't come over. But he said, "OK, come on by." *Voom*, man, I was over there quickly. His place was in a very small apartment complex in Beverly Hills, not the ritzy houses. So I go over, he brings me into the house, and as I turned the corner from the entryway into the living room, there it was, on the wall....

SC And it had never twigged with him, even after you were calling him once a week?

RM No, he didn't really know and didn't really think like that. But Ron Borst's book *Graven Images* had been out, and I'd been to Ron's house, and ...

SC Who's Ron?

KH Ron Borst. He's another big collector. He has *Murders in the Rue Morgue*, *White Zombie*, a six-sheet of *Son of Frankenstein*—forty inches by sixty inches—the *Fu Manchu* insert. He was the first guy out [on the collecting scene].

RM Yeah, so anyway, *The Mummy* had been out and we were all familiar with that poster....

KH And it was accepted that that one was the only one known to exist.

RM Right. Nobody had ever seen this. So when I turned the corner and walked into that guy's living room and saw it, my old poker face finally fell. I mean, my jaw dropped massively. Suddenly it's "My God. It's the other one." It had never even entered my mind that it could have been the other one, because we didn't believe there was another one!

SC Right, so you got caught by surprise.

RM Very. It was laminated to a board, as it is now. That's the way it was found. And I got the whole story on it. The guy had been given this poster as a Christmas present from his parents. His parents had been given this poster, and a handful of others, as Christmas presents from a friend of theirs they'd gone to college with back in 1959, up at the University of Chicago. I asked if he would ever consider selling it, and he said no, it wasn't even up for discussion. A few months later, I showed up with $10,000 cash on me, laid it out on the table, just to let the guy know I was serious, and he flipped out completely. He screamed, "What are you doing? Get that money off my table. Are you crazy, walking around with money like that? Get it outta here. Get it outta here." He was very set. "It was a Christmas present. I cannot sell Christmas presents." So this is what I was up against. I started thinking, how could I get him to sell it? And I felt that if his parents said sell it, then because they're the ones who gave it, that would work. So I went to the parents. On their wall they had an original one-sheet for *All Quiet on the Western Front*, which was the Best Picture of 1930.

KH Another very desirable movie poster....

RM Only one other copy of that is known to exist. I was losing my mind! This was incredible!

Now, these people were really nice people and they were saying, "Yeah, we'd love to sell it to you but we can't because it was a Christmas present." I asked who they got it from, and they gave me the guy's name, who was in Chicago. But of course he does winters in Mexico, so I'm calling the U.S. consulate in Mexico, trying to track this doctor down in Mexico....

SC This is like an insane detective story.

RM Oh, it took months. Months. Anyway, I had to wait until the spring. And finally the guy came back to Chicago, and I called and asked him the story behind how he got 'em, and he had gone antiquing with a friend of his one weekend while they were at the University of Chicago.

And he says, "I remember going to this guy's house and he remodeled furniture, and on the back of his lot he had a, like a big barn. So we went out there, and lining the whole row of the barn were stacks and stacks of old movie posters. He was just asking a dollar apiece for 'em, so we went through one of the stacks and we pulled a few out that we liked and bought 'em and left."

So I asked him what else he got, and he explained that he gave most of them to family and friends as Christmas presents! And he gave me some recipient names, which was amazing since it was back in 1959 that he had given these posters out. I called all those people up, and they still had the posters! These people had been given 'em but no one would sell them, and some of them were OK but there were a couple of really good ones in there, too.

KH (turns focus to Ron directly) Like what?

RM There was a *Ladies They Talk About*, Barbara Stanwyck, 1933. The poster was designed by Alberto Vargas. I mean, this guy had an eye for quality posters in 1959. So—and he still had some in his attic. So he said, "I'll go up in the attic when it warms up a little bit and I'll call you when I find what I still have." He still had two *She Done Him Wrong* one-sheets from Mae West. I asked if he could remember the town he went to. He couldn't, but he remembered the guy he was *with*, so I proceeded to track *this* guy down. And after some prompting, he remembered the place, the barn, but by the time I got to him I was too late by a month, he'd passed away. So I talked to his sons, and they said, "Oh yeah, all those stacks and stacks of movie posters?" I excitedly said, "Yes!" And they replied, "We have no idea what happened to those." So somewhere out there! ...

SC That must have been frustrating.

RM Well, yes. It could have been one of the greatest finds of all time.

SC And let's get back to how you got your man to cough up the poster.

RM Right. So I told the doctor in Chicago that I'd called this family in Los Angeles and I was trying to buy this *All Quiet on the Western Front* from 'em, and I've offered 'em a lot of cash for it, but they didn't feel right because it had been a gift! And he goes, "God, they should sell that!" I asked if he would please call them and say that, he agreed, and the next day, the parents call me asking, "Hey, still want that *All Quiet on the Western Front*? Come get it." So I went over there with a pile of cash and bought it from them. Then I said, "You know what I'm gonna do for you? I'm gonna make you an absolutely perfect copy of this, so you can put it on your wall. Don't hang anything up there, I'll do it the exact same way." So I went down, had it photographed, had it enlarged full size, had it mounted, laminated to a board the exact same way they had had it, took it over and hung it on the wall for 'em. They were excited. And *then* I said to them, "You know, I've been trying to talk to your son about *The Mummy* one-sheet he's got, but he said it's a Christmas present!" So they called him, and sure enough, I got a call from him the next day asking if my offer for the poster was still good, and if so, to go on over and get it. Which I did. And that's how I got it. I also made him an exact copy of it and hung it on the wall the same way.

SC It seems like you have all shared similarly disjointed childhoods? Childhoods where, for whatever reasons, you felt like the outsiders? Maybe childhoods where you're—

KH Oh yeah, I know how to talk to these guys. Ron and I speak their language because we are one of them. If you can relate to these guys on their level, and speak their language and vocabulary, it's gonna make that much more of a difference because, first of all, they're gonna trust you, and second of all, they're gonna know that you know what you're talking about.

SC And even though you say that they don't care about who you are with respects to being Metallica's guitarist, nonetheless when they do find out, it must be great. Because there you are, a huge famous musician but also one of them, the King of the Outsiders.

KH Absolutely, and I'm well aware of that. Put it this way, I hate using the word "nerd" now because the hipsters are now nerds. I come from a more traditional, genuine nerd sort of thing.

You know that movie *Revenge of the Nerds*? Well this is revenge of the nerds in reality right here, *me!* But anyway. I'm the nerd who turned it around and didn't desert my tribe.

SC And it is quite a tribal community.

KH Yeah, it's like a little social club that not very many people are allowed into. And if you say you "are," then people want to see proof that you actually are the person that you claim to be. There are still collectors out there I've never met that I know all about. I know what they have. But they just don't want to know me. They're just not interested in meeting me for whatever reason.

SC Maybe because of the rock 'n' roll side of your life, they think you're not a "serious" collector.

KH Yeah, it sometimes works against me. More than a few times I've heard "I'm not doing any business with that rock star. I'm not selling anything to him. That rock star can kiss my butt because he bought a poster I was trying to get three years ago."

SC And they think you're doing it just because you can. They don't know you're doing it because you love it.

KH You know, I'm sure that probably comes into the argument or their reasoning at one point or another. But I love it. The people I deal with are just eccentric. They're not trendy and they're not hip. If anything they are the nerds that they always have been and always will be. They're real. They mean it. And I relate to all of them in that way. And that's the thing with the idiosyncratic world of collecting; it has its cloak-and-dagger moments even though it's just a bunch of nerds. But we all understand the world we live in, and that constant wait for the next discovery drives us all!

FORREST J. ACKERMAN

Forrest J. Ackerman was a huge influence on me. As the editor and guiding force behind *Famous Monsters of Filmland* you felt his presence in every issue. His wacky sense of humor and bad puns were pervasive throughout, and something I looked forward to eagerly every four weeks. Forrest was a true pioneer of collecting movie posters, props, books, artwork. And whenever pictures from his house (the Ackermansion) were shown in the mag, I would sit and marvel at all the incredible items pictured on his walls. AND he always looked like he was enjoying himself immensely!

A monster kid like myself would dream of getting a chance to meet Forry, and I finally did in 1987! I even got to go to a local diner to eat pie with him! I kept up a loose correspondence with him over the years — he came to see one of our shows in 2004! — and when he passed away in 2008, at the ripe old age of 92, it was a sad day for all of us monster kids — mostly now monster adults — and a sad day for fandom as well. But as you can clearly see, his spirit and influence live on!

These were some of the
earliest toys from the
'60s, right before the
monster craze really
kicked in. Anatomical
toys were given a
monster spin to them.
And Horrible Herman
was just a feathery
plastic thing that you
manipulated via a hole
in the bottom of his box.

THE GREAT GARLOO AND
THE GREAT SON OF GARLOO

Who can control this terrible monster? You can, kids! With the
remote control you were able to make him go forward and backward.
He was able to bend down and move his arms together to pick things
up as well. I'm glad that the Great Garloo was able to procreate so
that we could have the Son of the Great Garloo around as well. But,
being an infant, he was restricted to walking.

BOBBLEHEADS!

These headbanging monsters are cool caricatures. This very Frankenstein bobblehead I once saw in FJA's basement in the dirt. I guess someone eventually fished it out and had Forry sign the bottom of the base...

PORCELAIN

Purportedly, these figures were sold at the Universal Studios gift shop. Notice how Frankenstein's monster is a little vertically challenged, compared to Drac and Wolfie! And Wolf Man's base says "Castle Dracula" while the monster's says "Mighty Monster"!

YETI THE ABOMINABLE SNOWMAN AND KING KONG FIGURE

Despite his bad moustache, the Yeti has a scream that put to shame King Kong's obsessive chest pounding!

FRANKENSTEIN HORROR TARGET

Made by Hasbro. Styrofoam balls were thrown
at a cool portrait of Frankenstein's monster on
a backboard. I think the Old Dark House on the
packaging is great as well ...

MONSTERS ARE GOOD CLEAN FUN

These figures were filled with children's bubble bath and were called "Soakies." Observe the vividly detailed blood on the mummy, the blood on the Wolf Man's face, and the fish in the Creature's hand!

HAUNTED HOUSE SOAP

I love that the color of the soap is "Frankenstein Green." The box shape reminds me of an outhouse!

MONSTER BUTTONS

Full-color illustrations of monsters inspired by the Aurora monster box artwork and *FM* magazine make these buttons very cool. The smaller black-and-white versions are part of a vending display card.

FRANKENSTEIN ROALEX PUZZLE

I could never finish this puzzle as a kid.

MONSTERS HORRORSCOPE SLATE

The header card for this toy has a funny scene of a sick Franky being visited by the other monsters. The Creature is tickling his feet, which have bolts!

BLOODY MARY, ANYONE ?

Let's have a Mad Monster Party! Oh wait, us monster kids are too young to drink! Where's Dr. Jekyll when you really need him?

The horror scenes on these puzzles are really out there! The Dracula puzzle has a dog with a human head. The mummy puzzle shows a lizard eating a man. Frankenstein shows a scene from *Frankenstein Meets the Wolf Man* as well as a hypodermic needle, and the Wolf Man puzzle features an Aurora-inspired version of both the Wolf Man and Frankenstein's monster. The promotional poster to the left has a drawing of the Glenn Strange monster.

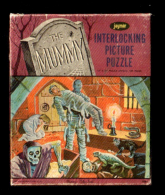

"MEET MY PAL
the MUMMY." says
Frankenstein's monster
on the front of these very
desirable Phoenix Candy
boxes. I wonder if the ad on
the bottom of the mummy
box is still valid?

IT'S ALIVE!!!

These rubber band-powered
Tricky Walkers, made by
Jaymar, are super rare. To
get them in the box is close
to impossible! Interesting
expression on Drac's face,
kinda like "What's that
smell?"

DARK ART

Painting by Numbers was fun until you eventually got all the paints mixed up together. Then your colors would go from normal to wacked out across the course of the painting! The Phantom paint kit seems Aurora inspired. If anyone has a Creature Painting by Numbers set, contact me at kirk@tmhb.com.

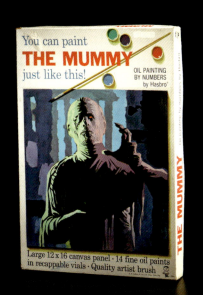

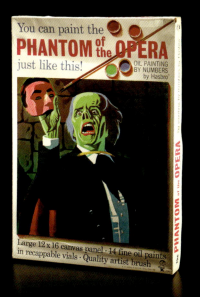

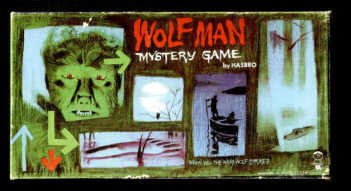

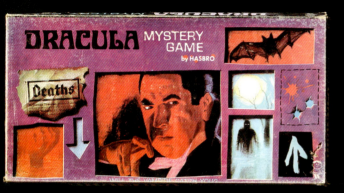

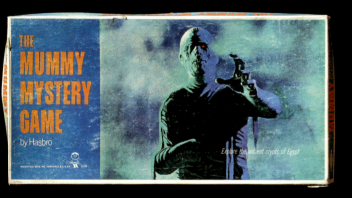

MONSTER MYSTERY GAMES

Hasbro, the makers of the Painting by Numbers kits, made these games as well. I suspect that the mummy and the Phantom games came out around the same time as the Mummy and Phantom Painting by Numbers kits. They share similar graphics.

THE PHANTOM OF THE OPERA MYSTERY GAME

In 1957, James Cagney portrayed the Phantom, and it's fascinating to me that this Bud Westmore makeup job would be the predominant image for Phantom toys in the '60s. Of them all, this game has the coolest graphics!

BORIS KARLOFF'S MONSTER GAME

Boris Karloff had a popular TV show in the '60s called *Thriller*, and this game was released to capitalize on the success and image he portrayed as the host. I think the box art is killer!

KING KONG AND GODZILLA BOARD GAMES

Out of all the monster board games, I seem to like these two the best. Wanton destruction of whole cities with the throw of a dice! Other than the model kit, this was the very first Godzilla toy to appear on the scene in the '60s!

AURORA
MONSTER MODELS

These models were instrumental in kicking off the entire monster toy craze in the '60s. The mummy, Dracula, and Frankenstein's monster pictured here were factory painted models sent to hobby stores for display. The Forgotten Prisoner model was painted by myself, circa 1987. The Vampire model was a collaboration between William Castle (director of movies such as *The Tingler* and *House on Haunted Hill*) and Aurora to make a less-horrific line of monster models; this female vampire was the first one to be issued.

AURORA MONSTER MOBILE

The Aurora box art is synonymous with '60s monster toys in general. They were the template for a lot of offshoots and revisions of other monster toys for years to follow. Painted by James Bama, reinterpretations of these images ended up on posters, puzzles, games, wallets, plaques, etc. ... Pictured here is a mobile used to promote the monster models in hobby stores.

THE CREATURES FROM THE BLACK LAGOON

Pictured from the left are two factory-painted display models, with the original sculpture used to make the master mold of the actual Creature model! Notice the sharper detail on the Gillman's skin and face.

MARX WALKING FRANKENSTEIN

Like Great Garloo before him, this Frankenstein toy could walk forward and backward, bend over, and pick things up. What potential! The head sculpt on the toy as well as the box art both show an excellent depiction of the Glenn Strange Frankenstein monster.

MONSTER WALL PLAQUES

These plaques are amazingly hard to come by, so I was so psyched when I managed to acquire the Creature in the original package. That's one of my favorite pieces, along with the mint-in-package Phantom wallet.

This was one of the items I wanted most when I was a kid. When a full box was found in the Midwest in the mid-'80s, I couldn't believe it! The "movie" is basically a flip-book that you place in the viewer, turn the crank on the side, and watch. A sequence of pictures moving left to right, which were slightly different on each page, created movement when you "flipped" through them. The movies were scenes from the classics, but with different titles like "Dracula's Return," or "Frankenstein's Revenge." A very cool and original toy design!

"Knock Down the Horribles!" This series of monster figures by Multiple Products Co. went through different versions and repackaging over many different lines of toys. I think the packaging they created was as good as the toys themselves! The graphics on the box of the Horror House Target Set and the Weird Monsters Set remind me of pre-code '50s comic art.

PALMER MOVIE MONSTERS

This set has such an unusual choice of movie monsters — Gorgo. It! The Terror from Outer Space. King Kong with Fay Wray. the Cyclops from *The 7th Voyage of Sinbad*. as well as Frankenstein. Dracula. the Creature. and Wolf Man in a suit! The header cards on these packages are some of the best. Psychedelic Frankenstein head? Solid! Franky walking Gorgo on a leash? Classic!

HAUNTED HULK

The Horror of the Seven Seas is one of the rarer MPC toys, and it's even more rare in the original box. The blood-splattered sail and disembodied Phantom-like head make this toy look like it would be a rather rousing good time in the tub! Check out the black skulls and giant spider — so bizarre!

THE HORROR OF THE SEVEN SEAS

HAUNTED HULK

BIG FRANKIE

Big Frankie was a toy that went to market as a model, but I can't picture him on the runway, can you?

Even though he was marketed as an Aurora model, he was really a toy with movable arms. Sculpted in a style now known as super-deformed, he was the most accurate depiction of the Karloff monster of any of the monster toys of the '60s.

The Big Frankie knockoff figure in the background is a rare blow-molded Mexican "bin" toy, with a coin slot so it could be used as a bank.

PEZ MONSTER DISPENSERS

I can still taste that fizzy, chalky Pez flavor to this day. Shown here are the highly stylized vending machine boxes that came with the aforementioned Pez ...

HALLOWEEN PARAPHERNALIA

This orange Frankenstein Halloween bucket is from the same mold as the Frankenstein head speaker below. The pencil sharpeners and Frankenstein and Dracula pipes are blow-molded toys made for mass production. Why kids would need plastic pipes on Halloween is beyond me!

FRANKENSTEIN HEAD SPEAKER

One of the more iconic pieces of monster toy collecting, to come across the Frankenstein head speaker with box is very uncommon. The graphics are hilarious. I wish I could be as cool as the monster kid on the box, walking around to the hip sounds coming out of the head speaker under my arm!

THE MAD MAD MAD SCIENTIST LABORATORY

Very cool chemistry set, with ingredients like "Ghouls Globules," "Skeleton Powder," "Mummy Crystals," and "Leeches Love Dust." Even though this was manufactured by a company called Chemlab, it's packaged exactly like an Aurora model, right down to the font and color scheme!

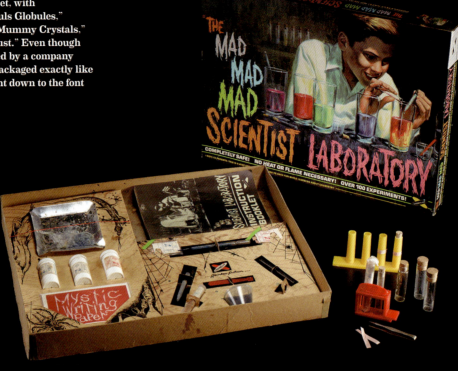

MONSTER PRINT PUTTY

A ghoulish version of Silly Putty, this toy came with a mini comic to lift images off with the putty.

MANI-YACK IRON-ON TRANSFERS

Really great iron-on decals for T-shirts, but I always wondered why the Creature was blue and Drac purple?

LIFE-SIZE MONSTER PIN-UPS

Two spectacularly graphic renditions of Frankenstein and Dracula. Franky is a bit bloody, while Dracula is baring his fangs for all to see! These two posters are over six feet tall, hence the "pin-up" tag.

HOOTIN HOLLOW HAUNTED HOUSE

This is one haunted toy! Set up with typewriter-like keys to trigger various actions, you had bats, black cats, and a vampire, all taking up residence in this wonderful tin litho toy. The box is equally fun, with the skeleton fleeing this too-scary household!

In 1964, *Famous Monsters* magazine announced its "Master Monster Maker Contest" in conjunction with Aurora models, ostensibly to push their two new customizing kits and monster paint products onto the monster toy market. The poster below was the initial ad that ran in the magazine. The winners of this contest were chosen by FJA, and received a plaque and a certificate commemorating their monster model building prowess. The plaque is amusing in that it is a replication of the Glenn Strange Frankenstein seen on the poster, and the end result is quite different. It looks like he's smoking a stogie!

CREATE AND DRAW MONSTERS

This toy is an electric tracing desk that enables you to trace anything that is already drawn. Cool illustrations on the box of some different-looking monsters. I like the monster kid the most!

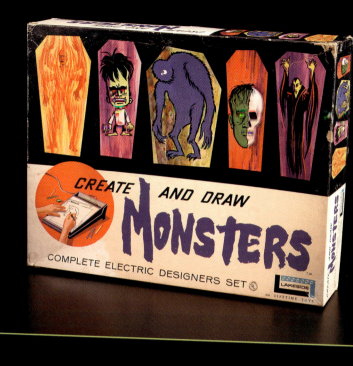

FORMEX 7 CASTING SET

Formex 7, better known as "wax," was heated and poured into molds shaped like the classic monsters, so at the end of the day you had your own little horror wax museum!

MINI-MONSTER SCULPTEES

Made of paper, these Sculptees were more like paper dolls than actual sculpted toys. The packaging with the Old Dark House in the background is a favorite motif of mine — I like anything that has it!

JAPANESE MONSTER VEHICLES

The cars on the left were wind-ups that walked rather than rolled. The sculpt on the Dracula is one of the best depictions of Lugosi, while the Frankenstein looks truly like a combination of the Glenn Strange/Karloff monster! The "Groolies" car is another cool Japanese item, with Frank driving Mr. Hyde, the Wolf Man, the female vampire from *Blood of Dracula* (!??), and Dracula in the rumble seat waving good-bye! When you wind the car up, it kind of "shimmies" across the floor!

A STRANGE CHANGE TOY

I had this toy when I was a kid, and I can tell you that it was one of the best toys of my childhood! Plastic squares would be heated up, and after they were warm enough, the squares would turn into little figurines of dinosaurs, skeletons, and various other creatures. When you were done, you could put them into the "compression chamber," which was a vise-like hand crank that squished them back into square form. Hours of fun!

INFLATABLE VINYL MONSTERS

These Japanese inflatables are so elusive that I only found these three just recently! The header card is remarkable to me because it has an illustration of what would appear to be the Dick Smith makeup for the TV version of *The Picture of Dorian Gray*, an image that was printed regularly in *Famous Monsters* magazine. Why they chose to put that on the packaging is beyond me, but I like it!

BIKE FLAPS AND ACCESSORIES, MONSTER STYLE

Customize your bike with monsters! The bike buddy was something you would mount on the handle bars so that you would never ride alone! The bike flaps were too cool to use as mud guards. I would have used them as necklaces!

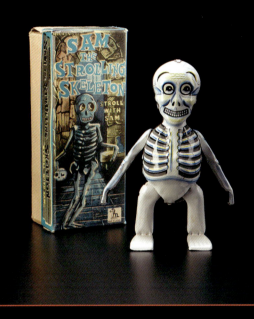

SAM, THE STROLLING SKELETON

When this guy was wound up, he would stroll in a fashion that reminds me of too many strolls to the bar!

WALKING FRANKENSTEIN AND WOLF MAN MODEL KITS

Made by Okamoto models in Japan, these two kits are the rarest monster models, period. To have both models with the boxes is seldom seen. In Japan, Frankenstein and the Wolf Man are viewed as fifty-foot creatures, so, like Godzilla, if they're that big, they have got to be able to breath fire, right?

WITCH DR. HEAD SHRINKERS KIT

NOW, SHRUNKEN HEADS FOR ALL OCCASIONS! Whew, I was getting worried about what I was gonna do for Arbor Day... What is it with shrunken heads? Kids go nuts for these withered talismans, I know I did! You would mix the powdered flesh with water, pour it into the mold, pull the head out and paint it, then overnight you would find that your head had shrunken down to half its size! Brilliant!

BLUSHING FRANKENSTEIN

One of the most original and brilliantly crafted monster toys of the '60s. You press a button, the monster would raise his arm and take a step, and then HIS PANTS WOULD FALL DOWN, revealing striped underwear and a blushing Franky! I had this when I was a kid, and I would get so much joy out of showing all the adults around me and hearing them laughing hysterically afterward!

THE THINGMAKER FRIGHT FACTORY

This toy was *sooo* übercool when I was younger. I would sit there and bake up skeletons, fangs, oversize eyes, shrunken heads, scars, and whatnot, and when I ran out of the plastic goop that was used to make these things, I would use the heating element to melt my army men! The graphics on the Skeletons Accessory Kit rule!

WIGGLE-ICK MONSTERS

It really is amazing, the decisions a manufacturer might make, sitting around a desk, wondering what characters to turn into toys. For this particular line of bobble heads, it was the Phantom (pretty standard), the Creature (also pretty standard), the It! The Terror from Beyond Space (Palmer Toys beat them to it, which makes it a weird choice), and FRANKENSTEIN'S DAUGHTER! It just makes me think — what an abstract choice! Was it because they actually liked this (famously bad) movie?

This was the debut of glow-in-the-dark plastic in toys, and what better than to use the
Aurora monster models as their testing grounds?

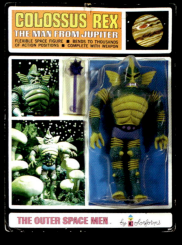

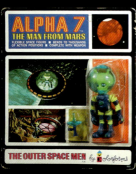
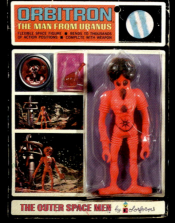

COLORFORM ALIENS — THE OUTER SPACE MEN

Major Matt Mason was a line of astronaut and space toys that was immensely popular in the late '60s.
This line of aliens was made as an accompaniment to Major Matt Mason as they were made in the same
scale. But that's where the association ends, because these aliens were WAY COOLER! They each came
with their little tools or weapons, and you can see where the designers got their inspiration from. Orbitron
looks like the Metaluna Mutant from *This Island Earth*. Electron looks like the Martian from *The Man
from Planet X*. Alpha 7 looks like the alien from the movie *Wizard Of Mars*. Colossus Rex (my favorite!)
looks like a monster from a certain Frank Frazetta painting. All in all, a very unusual line of toys from
Colorform, very cool and rare to find mint in package!

MARX MONSTER FIGURES

The Marx Monster Figures feature some of the best sculpting jobs of all the figures from the '60s. The Creature, mummy, and Wolf Man are especially good!

MOTORIZED MONSTER MAKER

Again, this toy was a Christmas present I had when I was a little ghoul. I suspect that it was made in response to the Thingmaker line of toys, but these were next level because you could bake the parts with goop, assemble and paint them, then put it all together on a body that had a wind-up mechanism built inside, so they could walk! The Mad Doctor always looked more wacky than mad to me, and Bobo Bones was not just your run of the mill, bucktoothed mummy, my friend!

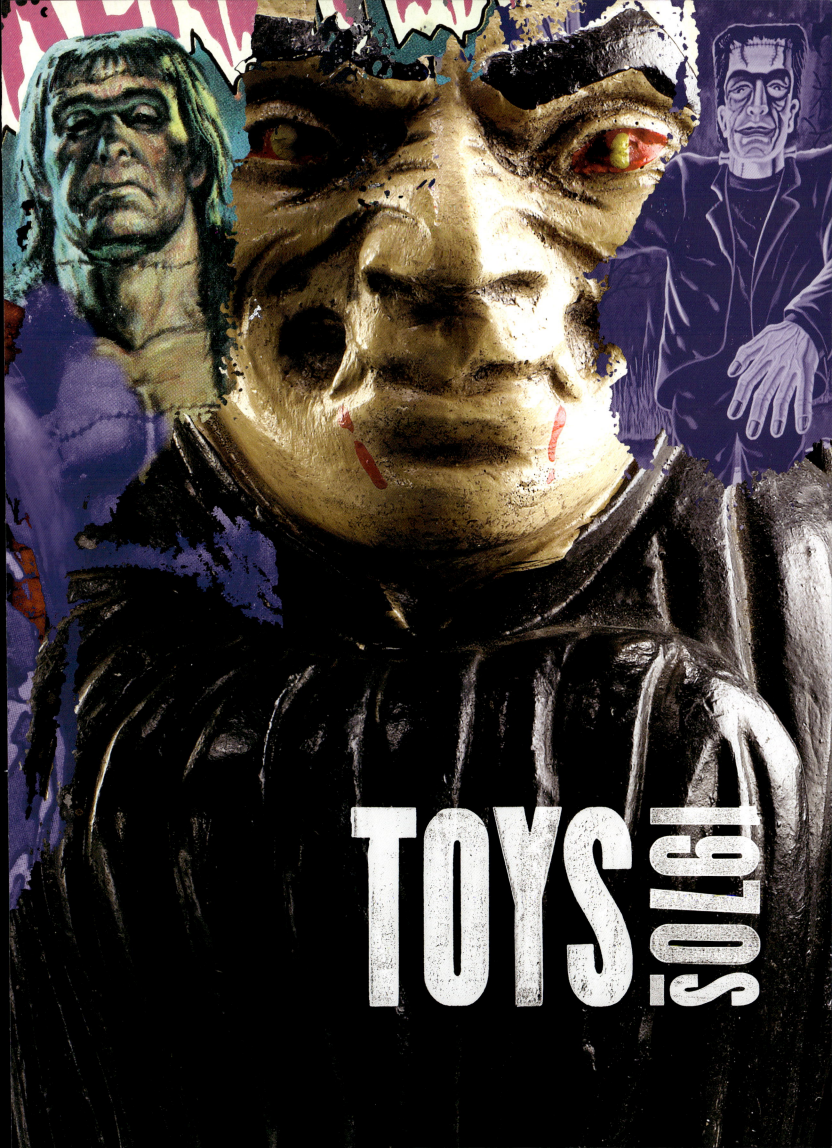

TOYS 1970s

PENN-PLAX
ACTION AERATING
MONSTER ORNAMENT

Have you ever seen those
mechanisms that pump air
bubbles into fish tanks? Well
this is one of them, but in a
Creature body! Also shown
here is a rare variation — a
BLACK Creature from the
Black Lagoon.

MONSTER SCENES

Monster Scenes were a very morbid and graphic line of kits. Aurora had to stop production because they were deemed too "sadistic and sexist." Pictured are the figures that came with this line of toys. Dr. Deadly's Daughter was previously known as "The Victim"!

GROOVIE GOOLIES

Is it any surprise that this was one of my favorite Saturday morning TV shows? I can remember watching it like it was just yesterday! The opening sequence showed footage of the Goolies playing as a band, and I just love that! Shown here is one of the figures in the counter display box, along with two puzzles.

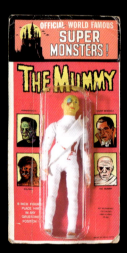

AHI MONSTERS

The AHI line of Super Monsters included action figures, jigglers, wind-up toys, bendies, and squirt guns! They were produced cheaply so that they could be sold at most five-and-dime and bargain stores, drugstores, and mom-and-pop places as well. The artwork for these toys is mostly dodgy, but that only adds to their charm! I would say that AHI made the definitive monster figures, the sculpt job on the Frankenstein monster looks like Karloff, Drac looks like Lugosi, and the Wolf Man is dressed like he just left a monastery! Shown at top are two Bend-'Ems and the counter display box they came in. The circular inset shows a walking King Kong, while to the right is the action figure line of monsters.

LINCOLN MONSTERS

Another entry in the monster action figure market were these Lincoln Monsters. These figures had a design aesthetic all their own — Dracula had blue mascara, the mummy had what seemed to be flashing red eyes and really, really bloody bandages, the Wolf Man was laughing about SOMETHING, and Frankenstein was lime green! Anyway, these figures are really hard to find, and the packaging is interesting in that it shows each Monster's various "scenarios"!

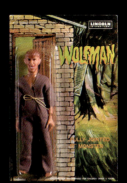

AHI MONSTER SQUIRT GUNS

Of course, if you are going to make a monster squirt gun, who would be your first choice? The Creature squirt gun is mighty impressive, I must say, while the Karloff monster head is a pretty darn good rendition!

MONSTROUS
MONSTER BISQUE

Someone just couldn't contain themselves and HAD to put a monster spin on the whole DIY arts-and-crafts movement in the mid-'70s. The poses on these three monsters look as if they are about to have a shootout. Notice that the Wolf Man keeps his gun in a different spot than the other two!

FAMOUS MONSTERS CANDLEMAKING SET

I wouldn't want to light these candles, because after putting all that time and effort into making and painting them, I couldn't just burn them! The mummy was exclusive to the four-pack.

FAMOUS MONSTERS PLASTER CASTING KIT

Now these are cool busts to look at, but as a kid in the mid-'70s, I was looking for something a little bit more action-packed.

SOME PEOPLE LIKE GARDEN GNOMES

But I like these two particular statues of Drac and Franky, and you rarely have a figure of Dracula with his cape closed.

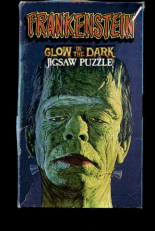

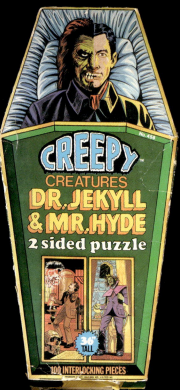

GLOW-IN-THE-DARK JIGSAW PUZZLES

Taken right off the covers of *Famous Monsters* magazine — I really like these glow-in-the-dark puzzles. When I look at them, it's interesting to see a different font where the *FM* logo would normally go.

CREEPY CREATURES JIGSAW PUZZLES

I once owned a couple of these and always appreciated the fact that they came in coffin-shaped boxes.

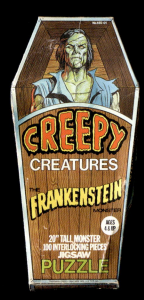

CONVENTIONAL MONSTER WISDOM

Here are some items from the first 1974 Famous Monsters Convention, a show that sounded like heaven on earth to a twelve-year-old kid like myself!

OIL PAINT BY NUMBER KITS

By the '70s, the Aurora influence on monster toy packaging was long gone, as you can see with these paint kits. The presentation is bare bones here (no pun intended). Also, notice the Phantom illustration is more of a watered-down mix between Lon Chaney and the Aurora Phantom.

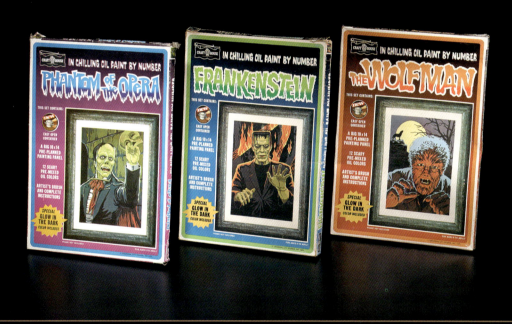

FAMOUS MONSTERS AND CREATURES

So the only real influence in the monster toy market must have been *Famous Monsters*, because this manufacturer just blatantly swapped the logo for their own product! With this toy you get a super bonus — a plastic creepy spider!

These two bigger-than-life monsters, along with Godzilla, were always a big hit with me when I was a pup. I remember having these two models when I was younger; I would only build the monsters so I could have fun with them, leaving the bases untouched in the box!

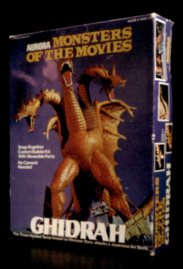

MONSTERS OF THE MOVIES

After the whole monster scenes debacle, Aurora decided to release a completely new and updated version of the classic horror monsters. The models were slightly smaller and had a little bit more detail to them, with completely different packaging. The approach to the models' poses was different, too, the best one being the Creature positioned so that he looked like he was swimming through water!

CREATURES FROM OTHER WORLDS

This was part of a line created to compete with all the new sci-fi toys that started to appear on the market around the release of the first *Star Wars* movie.

FAMOUS MONSTERS OF LEGEND

When I first saw the Cyclops when I was younger. I freaked out. thinking that it was part of a series that was somehow connected to *FM* magazine and the artist of this monster coloring book I once had. Turns out it was neither. and these figures were made by a knockoff company trying to grab a part of the monster action figure market. I think this was a cool choice of characters to produce. the Cyclops and the Fly being particularly cool!

CREATURE FEATURES: THE GAME OF HORROR

This game was produced to capitalize on the popular Creature Features TV shows across the nation. It plays like monopoly, but starring the classic monsters!

THE MONSTER GAME

I love the fact that this is a game that brings Frankenstein's monster back to life right on his own table!

POP-UP FRANKENSTEIN

The reason why I like this toy is that the head sculpt on the Frankenstein is done well!

SCARE CYCLES

The Scare Cycles are high up there on the coolness factor for mo! I lovod playing with the Evel Knievel motorcycle toy as a kid, and this monster toy version is just ultra mega great! Check out the cool sideburns that Franky is sporting!

RACK TOY MONSTER MANIA!

Rack toys were inexpensive toys that retailers could just put up on racks, no displays or extra marketing involved. It was a quick and easy way to have something to sell, especially around Halloween. Here are a few examples:

GLOW PUTTY

Silly Putty was such a great invention, the way it could be repackaged to suit any occasion!

YUK HEADS

The Jack Davis-inspired art on the card is fantastic! Looks like they made a Cousin Eerie and an Uncle Creepy Yuk head, too!

FLIPIT

I love the drawing on this toy, dig Franky's red pants and orange sweater!

FRANKENSTEIN FUN PONCHO

ALIEN

One cool toy for one cool monster! Apparently there was a big uproar when this toy came out — something about it being from an R-rated horror movie prompted complaints from parents. I personally think it's fantastic, being a big fan of the artist and designer H. R. Giger. It's great to see that one of his most monstrous creations made it into the hands of young kids everywhere!

As Seen
In the Movie!

ALIEN

Relive the Exciting Action of
ALIEN
with the Creature itself!

ANI-FORMS DRACULA AND FRANKENSTEIN

Dracula would rise out of his coffin and Frankenstein would break out of his straps by using pumped air from an inflator. A very clever toy that also glowed in the dark. I particularly enjoy the graphics on the Frankenstein box. It's the seldom-used Karloff monster from *Son of Frankenstein*.

MONSTER LUNCH BOXES

It took 'til the '70s for someone to figure out that kids needed a monster lunch box! Great cast of characters on this, the Wolf Man and the mummy look especially good!

ALIEN PUZZLE, MODEL, AND BOARD GAME

Because *Alien* was an R-rated movie, kids did not have access to the film, which in turn meant that interest in the toys would not be what it normally would have been. As a result, the entire line did poorly. So Alien toys from that era had low distribution. The puzzles and models did somewhat better, being geared toward an older demographic. On the board game, notice that a picture of the figure is on the box, rather than a picture of the Alien from the movie. I guess it was decided that this was less threatening for the kids who would be buying it!

REMCO MONSTERS

The Monsterizer is one of the coolest accessories ever produced! It gave you the perfect opportunity to become Dr. Frankenstein, or a mad doctor at the very least!

As the '70s drew to a close, it was evident that the monster craze was on its last legs. Public taste had shifted immensely toward a sci-fi sensibility, thanks to *Star Wars*' new and exciting possibilities, and the old classics were relegated to a crypt in some abandoned graveyard. This line of Remco monsters was the last attempt to get the most out of the action figure market, and it would only be a matter of time before the *Star Wars* franchise would dominate toys for the next ten years!

JAPANESE FRANKENSTEIN MODEL

Even though it says World Monster Series No. 1, it actually is the *second* series monster line that Okamoto put out. The presentation is more of a friendly Frankenstein than a foreboding one, unlike the previous series in the '60s.

JAPANESE TALKING DRACULA

This hilarious toy has eyes that light up, has a sinister laugh, and speaks with a slight Japanese accent. Very amusing to watch in the dark.

MECHA DRACULA'S COFFIN GAME

Kill the vampire! I love any game that has to do with impaling vampires with a stake ... Let's face it, it's fun!

TIME FOR A FAMILY PORTRAIT!

Here's a real rogues gallery of plaster and chalkware figures made by various companies like ESCO and Tuscany, among others. What makes these so appealing to me is all the different emotions that these figures seem to carry in their expressions, my favorite being the look of extreme ennui on The Wolfman's face on the right side of the page. I think it's stupendous that the manufacturers also did the Abbott and Costello meets Frankenstein figures. WITH a crate and straw, it's also a good thing I had an extra Frankenstein's monster hanging around to put in the crate!

MASKS

PROFESSIONAL, CUSTOM HAND-PAINTED
HOLLYWOOD MASKS!

Don Post was an innovator of over-the-head masks, which were made of really thick latex rubber. The series shown here is very endearing to collectors; these "Calendar Masks," as they are known, from a 1966 calendar that was sold in novelty shops, are prized for their accurate character representations, as sculpted by Pat Newman.

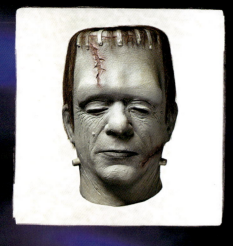

FRANKENSTEIN MASKS

Shown here are all the different variations of the Glenn Strange Frankenstein mask, arguably the best Frankenstein mask in production at the time. I only say that because some collectors prefer the Glenn Strange style to the original Karloff style. Personally speaking, I think Strange's facial structure made him more appealing as the monster. The top row shows the first style mask, partially based on a surviving headpiece Glenn wore in *Bud Abbott and Lou Costello Meet Frankenstein*. The bottom row shows a later resculpt by Pat Newman, both of which were offered in the mid-'60s.

CREATURE/MOLE MAN/ METALUNA MUTANT

Out of all the masks ever produced, the fact there were the Metaluna Mutant and the Mole Man was amusing to me, because they are not generally regarded as classic Universal monsters! I personally think the Mutant is especially cool and unique!

VERNE LANGDON ZOMBIE

The mask on the opposite page is a recast of a very rare mask that came out in the late '60s. In the hippie era, making a zombie mask with long blonde hair seems like someone was trying to make a bit of a statement on youth culture at the time ... at least to me it does!

TOPSTONE
MUMMY MASK

To the left, one of the best original mummy designs ever!

SAME MASKS USED BY WORLD-FAMOUS UNIVERSAL PICTURES

HORROR ZOMBIE MASKS

Horror Zombie was an iconic symbol in the '60s and was one of the definitive images of *FM* magazine, who used Horror Zombie as an official mascot in its early days, putting him on *FM* fan club material, as well as T-shirts and other merchandise. I love Horror Zombie. I think he encapsulates '60s monsterdom in a very fun and lighthearted way! I also think the inspiration for Horror Zombie came from the creature in the movie *I Was a Teenage Frankenstein*, as both had those similar traits of green skin and a bulging eye staring at you. Pictured in the right-hand column above are three modern interpretations of our pal, and as you can clearly see, he's not like any zombie you would see on the screen today!

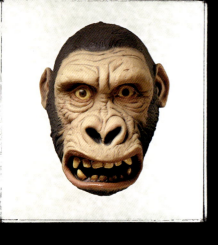

TOPSTONE MASKS

Topstone masks were the cheaper alternative to the high-quality Don Post masks, being made of thin rubber and not being over-the-head masks. But what they might've lacked in latex they made up for with character! They were designed by Keith Ward, the same illustrator who created Elmer the Cow on Elmer's Glue. The Melting Man, the Devil with a skullcap, the Green Ghoul, and the Girl Vampire were all very cool designs that you had to have, even if they were original characters and not movie monsters! These are actually recasts of the originals, but in a lot of instances they were "improved" by resculpting them, plus they were made with thicker rubber for better wear and longevity!

EXTRA ★

THE EVENING TIMES

ZACHERLEY FINDS MISSING
LINK IN JERSEY SWAMPS!

Panic In New York;
Menagerie Breaks Loose

English Sailor
Set Mark for
Marathon Walkers

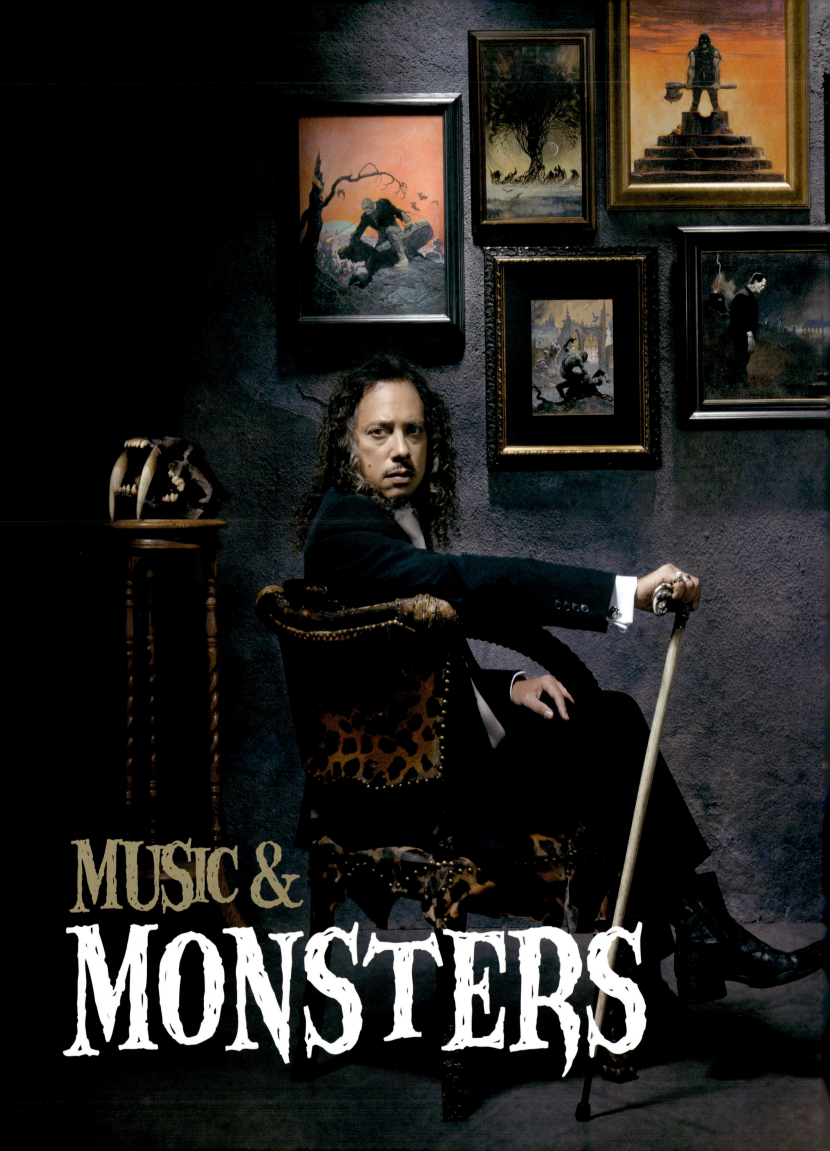

MUSIC &
MONSTERS

A conversation
with Kirk Hammett

Passion and expression often share the same root lineage. In Kirk's case, as he was being exposed to the world of monsters, toys, movies, and comics, he was also hearing the sort of irreverent sounds from his brother's stereo, which resonated heavily with him. The skull-laden art of many album sleeves from that era and the crazy images plus doomful sound of Black Sabbath were early ear- and eye-grabbers, while colorful geniuses such as Santana and Jimi Hendrix immediately caught his young teenage soul with their playing. Thus it wasn't long before Hammett found that he needed to speak as they did, with a guitar. Naturally, the reclusive young horror-loving riffer went on to become the lead guitarist (aka The

SHE LIVES!

Me and my Bride (of Frankenstein guitar!) in action with Metallica, during the *World Magnetic* tour, October 2009.

Rippёr) in Metallica, perhaps the world's biggest heavy metal band and a regular headliner in stadiums around the world. (And the geek shall inherit the earth, right?) But just when one might imagine the collecting game, and all this horror business, might have been a flight of childhood, Hammett found himself reconnecting with it more than ever ... in no small part thanks to the music. In our final conversation, at Kirk's San Francisco home, we discussed all aspects of how his collection and music found their dovetail ... or bat wings!

SC From what I can gather, music probably started coming into your world around the same time that you were painting model figures, before the real collecting urge took over.

KH Yeah. But music was more a part of the background. At my house, there was always a radio on or my brother was spinning his albums. And it was at that time in the 1960s and early '70s when all these great albums, and their respective cover art, were being released. I remember seeing gargoyles on the first Grateful Dead album, there was Hendrix's first and second albums, and Jethro Tull's first one, too. I was taking in all this imagery and was fascinated by it, particularly (for example) *Axis: Bold As Love* with all the deities behind Jimi Hendrix. I also particularly remember Santana's first album with the pretty famous, weird Mayan-like creature. I remember looking at the cover of Black Sabbath's *Paranoid* album and just laughing at it, like, "Who's this guy in his pajamas with a sword?" And I remember sitting in the living room on the floor, staring at these albums while my brother was playing them. I think I was subconsciously taking it all in and was just more interested in the graphics at the time.

SC So it was the images first, not the sound?

KH The imagery, definitely. One hundred percent.

SC It's interesting you mentioned the Grateful Dead. We think of them as trippy hippie, but all those skulls ...

KH The whole skull thing was a big part of how they represented themselves visually. But when I was fourteen, fifteen, in the late '70s, I was getting hip to the bands of the time, like Led Zeppelin, Pink Floyd, UFO, Thin Lizzy, Montrose, ZZ Top, and Lynyrd Skynyrd. I was finding my music; the music that spoke to me and took me somewhere, that made me feel the feelings I wanted to feel.

SC Which were?

KH Well, I should say it was just more emotionally fulfilling music. I was discovering my sound, and that sound was hard rock and heavy metal. When I started buying albums, I once again came across *Paranoid* by Black Sabbath. And I looked at the cover ... "Ah, I know this album, the guy in the pajamas again!" I opened it up, and there's the same picture of the four members that I recognized from my brother's copy years ago.

SC So you rediscovered it.

KH Yeah. But actually, the first music I rediscovered was Hendrix. I was at a rock concert when I was fourteen, and they were playing a recording of "Purple Haze" in between the acts. I said to my friend who was with me, "I know this song! I haven't heard this song in such a long time!" ... maybe since I was six or seven years old. Because by that time my brother, who's a lot older than I am, had moved out of the house. So I said to my friend, "I know this song," and his older brother, who was always the cool guy, said, "That's Jimi Hendrix. You should know that, what are you, stupid?" A light clicked in my head, and I went and bought the Hendrix album *Electric Ladyland*, and the *Woodstock* album, and started listening to Hendrix. Then I slowly rediscovered Sabbath, Cream, and Santana, and all these albums that my brother had listened to. But I discovered them through the music. Once I got the albums, I saw the imagery that I had connected with when I was younger. By that time I was already air guitaring, and it was only a matter of time before I bought a guitar and started playing for real. That was when my whole life changed.

SC You were fourteen?

KH I picked up a guitar about a month before my fifteenth birthday.

SC So let me ask this, because I think it's something that happens when you have a lifelong passion. There is always a period of time in your teenage years where something else takes priority for a little while. And would you say that, leading up to thirteen, fourteen, you were still pretty aggressively reading your monster mags and picking, buying toys, and—

KH Yeah, yeah, comic books. Yeah, and still watching all the movies. And for a brief time I got into model rocketry, but nothing really made an impression on me more than music. My whole life shifted, and for a while I stopped collecting. In fact, I started selling comic books and monster magazines to buy more records and began thinking, "I'm grown up now. I don't need this kid's stuff anymore." Instead, I bought heavy metal imports from Europe, and they were always more expensive because they were imports.

A figure in black. Me! I just love the vibe of this shot. It's dark, it's mysterious, it's an outtake but it's an outtake I thought was PERFECT for a heavy metal horror-loving guitarist!

SC So instead of passively engaging with comics and collecting toys, music became this thing that you could actually express yourself with?

KH Oh yeah, totally. To this day, playing the guitar is my ultimate means of creative expression. I see it as a limitless instrument to express myself in unlimited ways. And when I was fourteen, I recognized this right away in the guitar, and I was hooked. But in a way, when we moved from San Francisco to the suburbs, it was a little bit of a culture shock for me. I was a city kid, and kids in the city just had an attitude that was totally different from kids in the suburbs. And because of this, I became more of an introvert at that point. Which was when I discovered music and the guitar. I just thought, "What could be a better thing to do than just to sit in your room around a little record player, and play guitar!" You know, there wasn't anything like guitar magazines that had tablature that explained every single note that your favorite guitar player ever played. I mean, stuff like that didn't exist. Back then, all you had were the records. And when you did find the sheet music, it was very simplified. A lot of times it was only for piano, or it was just a chord. When a riff was played in E minor, they would just print the chord. You know, strum this chord while you're singing these lyrics. It was very simplified and just wasn't very good. So you had to do all the hard work yourself. You had to learn the hard way, which was by using your ear and hitting rewind, or in my case, picking up the needle and putting it back on the track or little section of the record, and playing it over and over again on your guitar until you found the notes and learned it. And see, it was the perfect environment because I felt like an outsider and wasn't really interested in making new friends, or any friends. I had a few friends here and there, John Marshall [former Metal Church guitarist] being one of 'em, and we sat in that little room of mine around that little record player and learned songs and eventually learned how to play guitar.

SC What's interesting is that you gravitated to the guitar and not to, maybe, drawing comic books or making films. Why do you think that is?

KH Actually, I've wondered about that myself, but I just think music's closer to my heart. It's my love. I mean, all this stuff is my love but music is instantly accessible to me.

SC And music is your voice.

KH Yeah, it definitely gives me a voice. I get such gratification just picking up my guitar, even if it's only for ten minutes. When I'm playing, maybe something magical might happen, and I think, "This is really cool, I'm really enjoying myself." And all of a sudden something else happens and there's a riff there or something, or I make a little

discovery, or I play something I've never played before. It's very soothing to fulfill that "need" to play, and the scenarios are endless.

And for me, it's a more instant language to express yourself with than making a film, which would take a long time, or drawing a comic book, which isn't really a language, it's an art. And after really finding what type of music I liked—loud, distorted guitar; big, banging drums; fast beats; slow, heavy beats—and then discovering heavy metal and seeing all this imagery, it just felt like second nature to me. I felt, "Oh, these are my people." You know, the first time I heard Black Sabbath, I knew this was the sound track of my life, right there. All that music, to me it was the sound track of so many horror movies. When I hear the beginning of "Iron Man," I don't really think of "Iron Man," I think of Universal monsters walking through my head. Seriously. So after seeing all this imagery around me, I met Cliff Burton [Metallica's original bassist] and he was also into that same sort of horror stuff. He loved zombies and knew about H. P. Lovecraft, which were great bonding things between Cliff and me. One of my greatest Cliff memories occurred about a week after I joined the band, when we had a night off. We were in New Jersey at the time, before we started recording *Kill 'Em All.* We crammed into two cars, got a gallon of vodka and some orange juice, a bunch of beer, and we drove to a drive-in and we watched *The Evil Dead,* which had just come out.

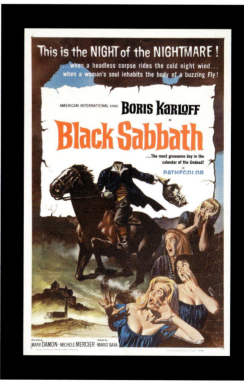

WHAT IS THIS THAT STANDS BEFORE ME?

How could any young, horror-afflicted kid resist either the movie or the band?

Behold! The toöls of The Rippër!

THE MUMMY GUITAR

The Rippër in action during Metallica's weeklong residency at San Francisco's Fillmore Auditorium, in December 2011, celebrating our thirtieth anniversary. Congratulations to us!

THE BAT LADY

This is a bronze art nouveau piece
from the turn of the century.
Sometimes I end up having a brush
with sophistication despite myself.

SC   Wow. Who drove?

KH   A friend drove one car and James [Hetfield] drove the other. I was so psyched because everybody was into it, and I thought, "Yeah, this is my tribe. These are my people." They don't really have to be freakin' horror fanatics, they just play heavy metal. And anyone who plays or listens to heavy metal understands horror movies, because it's all the same shades of dark and light. It's all made up of the same notes and the same molecules. They share a lot of the same ingredients, feelings, imagery, and thought.

SC   Do you think it's the voice of the outsider coming through again?

KH   Oh, totally. It's like you gave Frankenstein an electric guitar and he started playing guitar and got really good. Can you imagine him playing anything but heavy metal?

SC   Well, maybe goth.

KH   No, that's Dracula—he'd be the goth guy.

SC   You probably identified with goth music as well, right?

KH   Oh, absolutely. Sisters of Mercy. Bauhaus. Early, early Cult. And the Birthday Party. Leonard Cohen. You know, I like the Cramps. I like the darker stuff. Siouxsie and the Banshees, the Cocteau Twins. The Gun Club. Yeah, absolutely, goth appealed to me.

SC   But you were always gravitating to the outsiders. I mean, it was always about—

KH   The dark. The people who hang out in the dark

corners, those are my people. When I met my wife I instantly noticed that she was one of those people who hung out in the dark corners. Luckily I saw her!

SC   And so when you were comfortable enough as a musician, you started back up with the collecting.

KH   It was around the time when we came back from Europe. We'd just made *Ride the Lightning*. We took a break and had some time off, and I had a little bit of cash that'd come in. I went to a comic store, started buying up comics and monster mags, as well as looking in those monster mags at all those toys that I couldn't afford to buy when I was a kid. That was when I decided to start collecting vintage monster toys. It quickly became an obsession. Back then there was no eBay or Craigslist, just flea markets, garage sales, toy/comic conventions, and a lot of networking by word of mouth and phone. That's how you found collectables back then. It took a lot of hard work and commitment.

SC   Wasn't it around this time that the Misfits took a hold of you, too?

KH   Absolutely. One day Cliff Burton showed up, we started driving around, he put in this cassette tape, and he started screaming at the top of his voice like a lunatic. I gave him a funny look, thinking, "What the hell is wrong with this person?" I was taken aback by Cliff's little display of screaming and whacking the hell out of his cracked plastic VW logo steering wheel, using it as a snare drum and driving all at once. And I'm sitting there when he said, "Damn! I forget where we were going." And after the tape stopped, I said, "What the hell was that?" And he said, "Oh, it's the Misfits." I said, "Man, they're horrible." And he said, "F*** you." We got to wherever we were going, he brought the tape with him and immediately put it on inside. And as I listened to it again, I thought, "Hey, it's not bad. You know, it reminds me of the Ramones." And then once I saw the album I thought, "Hey, the Misfits logo is just like the *Famous Monsters of Filmland* magazine logo. And their skull is the one from *Crimson Ghost*, the movie serial from the 1940s." And then I saw what they looked like, and I thought, "Wow, these guys are totally using all this monster film, magazine, and comic book imagery and making it their own, really owning it." And I thought, "How cool is it that they're into monster movies," which was obvious from their lyrics. I thought, "These guys are completely supercool." At that point I understood where they were coming from visually, and it clicked with me that the Misfits were really horrible and really cool. When I heard the phrase "too much horror business," which is from a Misfits song incidentally, it resonated with me because I was diving headfirst into collecting again—too much horror business and not enough time! That was me, and, hey, that is me!

MISFITS DRUMHEAD AND CRIMSON GHOST LOBBY CARD

The drumhead was painted by Glenn himself in 1979, and above is the original Crimson Ghost image that was the basis for a lot of the Misfits' graphics.

WITH JOHNNY RAMONE

I look at this photo and can tell you exactly what Johnny and I were doing, which was referencing horror movies from the library of horror reference books you can see! I miss Johnny. I think he would've loved this book.

SC It became a beautiful thing.

KH Very much. They were God's gift to all the monster kids. And it was inspiring, too, because I could see that these guys were like me. They were into the same movies, toys, and comic books. And, when they got guitars, they put it all to music. They meshed it together. They melded it together. And I thought to myself, "Damn, why didn't I think of that?!"

SC But when you're sitting there writing music and thinking of the riff to "Enter Sandman," is it fair to say that all the years you spent watching these films as a kid have helped you find dark and angry riffs like that?

KH Oh, absolutely. I see and feel their shades and colors, which come through as dark and heavy riffs, because I've spent so much time with them my entire life. You know, it's my other world. And sometimes I put myself there, and sometimes I find myself there. It's a world of inspiration, and that's when I need to lunge for a guitar, or at the very least a tape recorder, and get that idea down on tape. Today, a lot of my inspiration comes from playing my guitar in front of these movie posters, seeing these incredible things that have colored my rich fantasy life. And you know, the beauty of these posters is that I love the contrast they show. I mean, that poster (*The Mummy* three-sheet) is a beautiful poster, but it's about a monster. It's about a horror movie. But look how beautiful it is! I enjoy that paradox greatly. When I first started collecting movie posters and I put up my very first *Bride of Frankenstein* half-sheet, it was really something, because it brought an element of beauty and historic significance into my collection. And it gave me a purpose—the purpose of needing to assemble these pieces together, so I can preserve, curate, and treat these things the way they should be treated, and eventually show them the way they should be shown, as great artifacts of twentieth-century horror cinema.

SC Have you ever found a like-minded collector friend in another band?

KH Johnny Ramone was a big collector of movie posters, and was very passionate about his collection. He was also well versed in the world of horror movies, although at the beginning, his emphasis was mainly on '50s and '60s horror and sci-fi ... until he saw my collection one day and decided to step it up considerably! After being inspired by seeing the depth of my commitment, he decided to follow suit and began collecting rare Universal horror items.

SC And thus a friendship was born, it would appear.

KH Oh yeah ... My wife, Lani, and I would go and visit Johnny and his wife, Linda, for days on end. We'd hang out, I'd help him acquire pieces for his collection, all the

while discussing the various merits and aspects of the posters, of collecting, and of the movies themselves. I really cherished the time I spent with him. I was a big Ramones fan from the very beginning and Johnny was one of my heroes, so it was amazing having a connection with him that had nothing to do with music.

SC So you were brothers in arms, perhaps?

KH Well, Johnny was a very complex individual. We didn't always see eye to eye on a lot of things, he was a bit conservative and contrarian on a lot of subjects, but the look in his eye always told me that he wasn't really serious about a lot of the things he said, and that he just liked getting a rise out of people. But when it came to horror movies, we were brothers in arms! I truly miss Johnny. He was the only other musician of prominence who I could share this passion with. He wasn't a poser. And whenever I acquire a cool item now, I always think about Johnny.

SC That's very cool ... Finally, let me ask you whether you see *Too Much Horror Business* as being a museum one day?

KH Well, the ultimate goal is to have it all out and on display, and to be able to share it with people. Hence this book. It's my way of sharing the best parts of it with everyone because it is just great, and I feel I can't keep it all to myself. I want to call people's attention to the grandiosity of horror movie poster artwork, and the wonderful kitsch factor of all those toys. I want the historic significance of all this beautiful stuff to be known, and I always wanted a book like this when I was a monster kid!

SC And this is only the greatest hits.

KH Yeah, there's still a lot of things that didn't make it in the book that should see the light of day sometime, and so I think, as in the tradition of any of those fine movie serials from the 1940s, it's: To be continued.

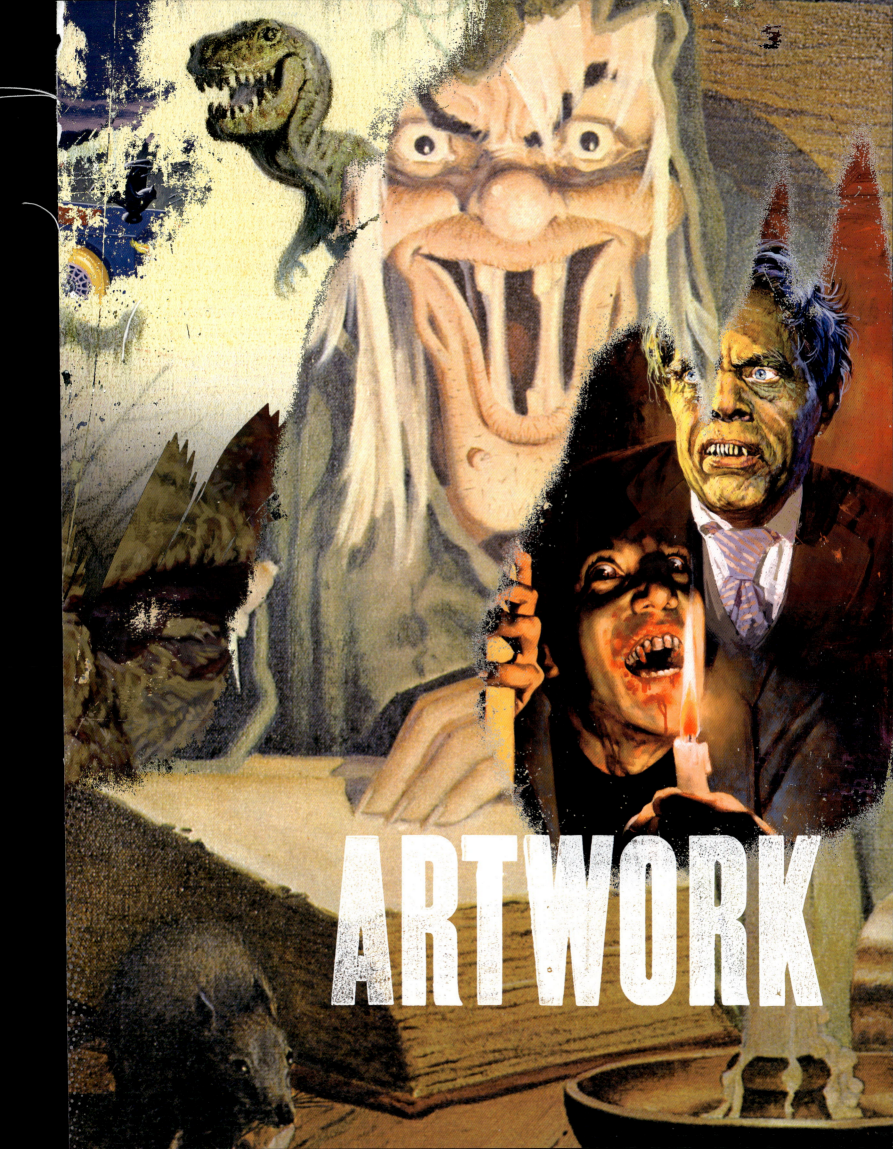

ARTWORK

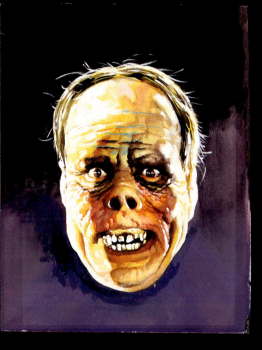

BASIL GOGOS — FAMOUS MONSTERS COVER ART

Jim Warren, publisher of *FM* magazine, demanded cover art that stood out from the crowd. And out of all the *FM* artists, Basil Gogos was my favorite. One of the brightest memories of my childhood was going to the newsstand to pick up the newest issue of *FM* magazine. I would always be in a state of anticipation as to which monster would jump out at me from the cover. I spent as much time staring at the cover as I did the inner contents! Gogos chose atypically bright-colored backgrounds for dark subjects (which made them pop), and maybe this was because he was in the middle of the '60s, and, well, those were the hippie days! When the opportunity came years later to buy some of these original paintings by Basil, and also by Ron Cobb (who went on to be a major Hollywood horror and sci-fi production designer on movies such as *Star Wars*, *Alien*, and *The Sixth Day*), I leapt at the chance! They remain some of my most prized possessions today. It would be negligent not to mention Russ Jones and Vic Prezio's artwork, as both also captured Jim's artistic ethic extremely well.

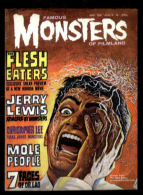

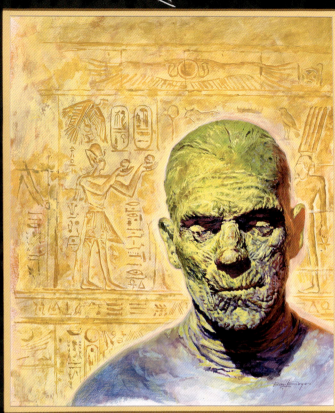

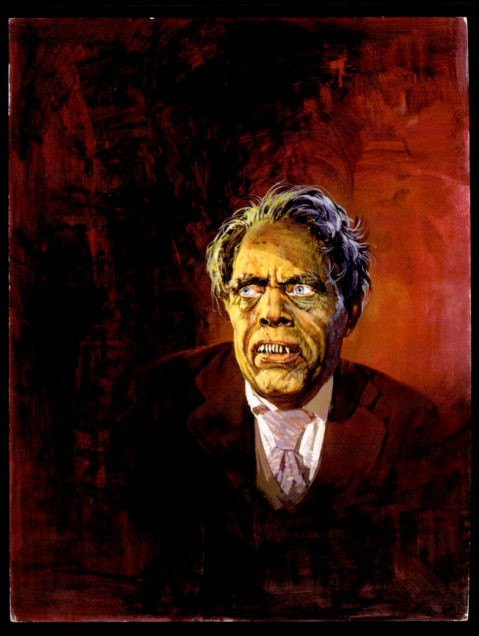

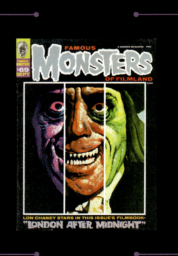

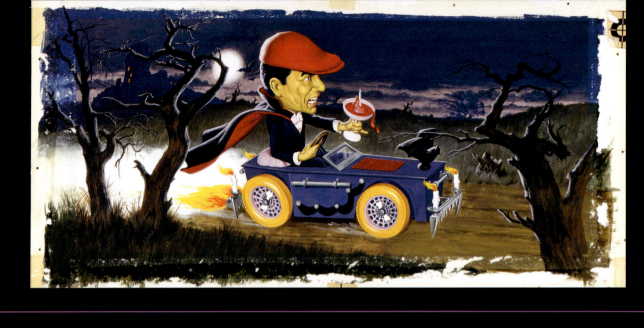

JAMES BAMA — AURORA MODEL PACKAGING ART

After I managed to score all those *FM* paintings, in 1992 I was approached by a prominent toy dealer who asked if I wanted to buy some Aurora models. I asked which ones were available, and he said, "All the monster hot rods!" I said I'd take 'em all! Funny thing is, I ended up with the paintings for the box art, by James Bama, before I got some of the kits themselves. It was great to have these paintings because Aurora models, and therefore the artwork on their boxes, were so much a part of my childhood. The monsters on the hot rod box art have always been my favorite of the whole series. Godzilla driving through a graveyard, Dracula drinking a martini with a staked heart in it while driving, Wolf Man cruising Norman Bates's house — all are just insanely funny send-ups of these normally austere classic monsters. I hope you enjoy the juxtapositions of this art as much as I do! After I'd scored the monster hot rods, the *Bride of Frankenstein* painting soon came into my life, disengorged heart and all. Also pictured is the original art from the Monster Scenes series. This came to me later, and I was fortunate to get artwork for the three main kits: Hanging Cage, Gruesome Goodies, and The Pain Parlor. It's unclear to me who painted the art for these immoral and sadistic children's toys … but I like it! It's easy to see why Aurora was a trendsetter in monster toy art and presentation.

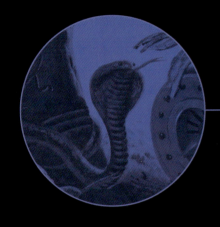

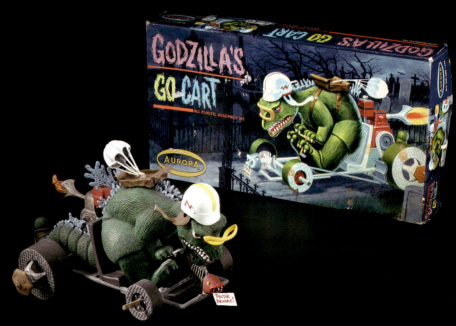

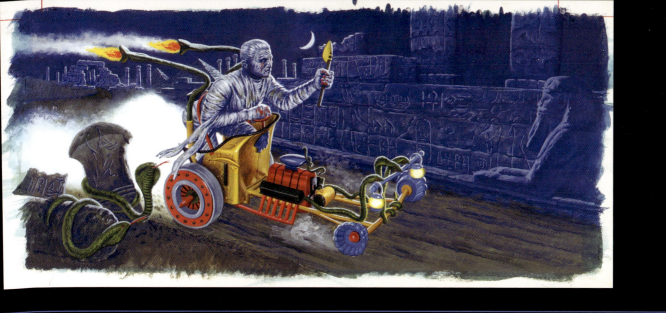

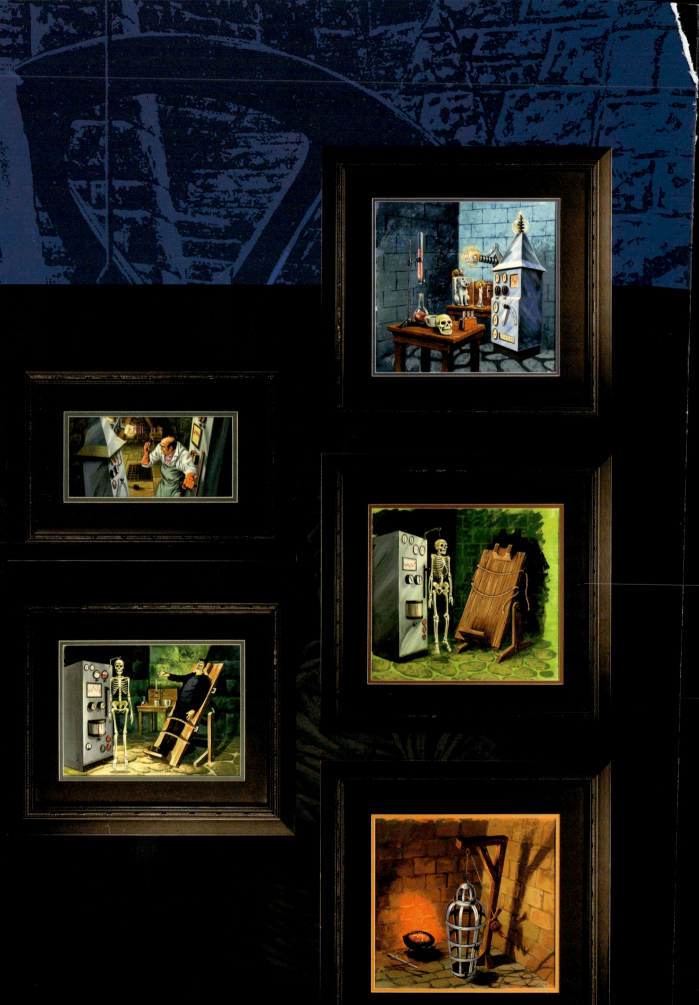

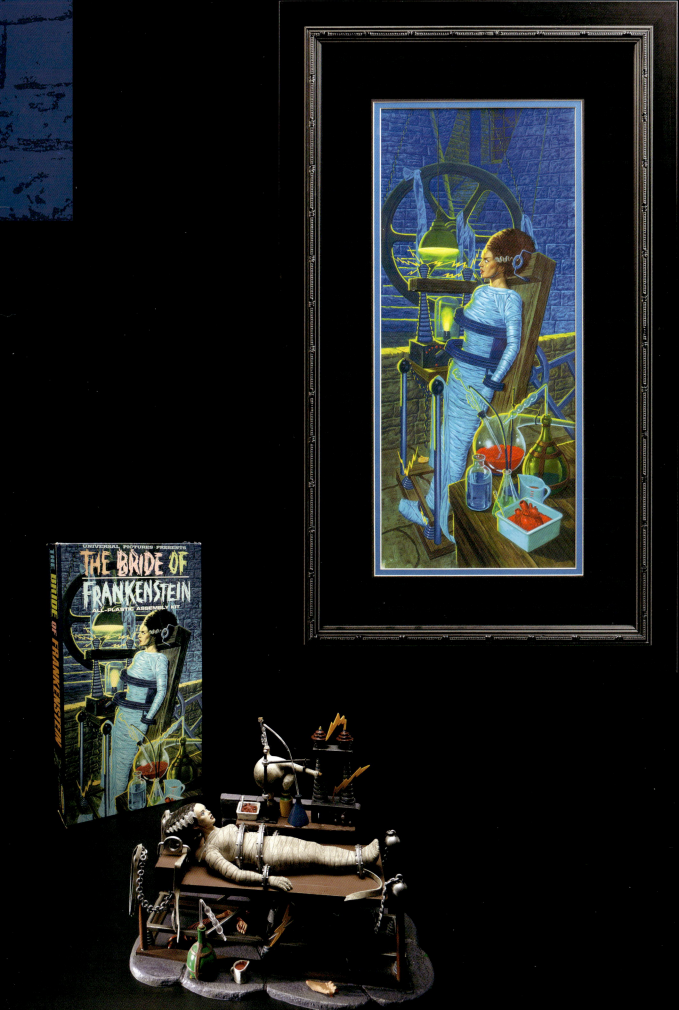

1. GLOSSY POS FROM 8½" TO 8⅜"   "WOLF MAN AND DRACULA" by Fraz

FRANK FRAZETTA

Frank Frazetta ... the Molly Hatchet cover art guy, right? Well, yes and no, because he was so much more than that. Frank Frazetta was God's gift (or was it from Satan?) to the world of illustration art. To me, he was a modern-day Michelangelo. His depictions of wizards and warlords, monsters and maidens, witches and werewolves (plus Conan the Beserker) pioneered the style for horror, fantasy, and sci-fi art. The first time I set eyes on his artwork, when I was around six years old, I could see it was the most evil-looking, the most sinister-looking, the stuff with the most depth, the stuff with the most demonic ingredients. His artwork just flowed at me in its seamless, otherworldly way, and the voluptuous, sexy women were a big part of Frazetta's style, too. His illustration of Vampirella, my ideal woman, was my first crush! His art always gave me a sense of wonderment, and Frazetta dependably stayed within the confines of good taste with whatever he did. I got to know this fine gentleman later on in life and was astounded to find out that he painted from memory (he never used a reference picture) and never spent more than a few days on any given painting, even his masterpieces. Frank Frazetta ... as you can see, so much more than just the Molly Hatchet guy!

TOP: DEAD OF NIGHT (1964)

LEFT: THE MONSTER MEN (1963)

RIGHT: THE EXECUTIONER (1967)

OPPOSITE PAGE:
CONAN THE BERSERKER (1967)

LEFT:
AUTUMN PEOPLE (1965)

RIGHT:
UNCLE CREEPY (1964)

BOTTOM LEFT:
CAT GIRL PREMIUM (1967)

BOTTOM RIGHT:
TERROR IN THE MIST (1959)

So I think by this point in the book it's pretty clear that my two favorite horror movie actors are Boris and Bela. I think that Boris is the better actor — he brings a certain creepy sophistication to a lot of the roles he's portrayed. But I think Bela had a much more interesting career as a whole, and because of this he seems more collectible to myself and a lot of other collectors. So here are some more Lugosi collectibles from the vaults!

DRACULA PARAPHERNALIA

Below: Pictured is Bela's personal copy of the script to *Dracula*. Shown are handwritten notes by Bela himself for the play *Dracula*, which he starred in right before the 1931 movie adaptation.

CERAMIC FIGURE

Right: Lugosi would gift these little ceramic figures of himself to friends back in the '40s. Only two or three have survived to this day.

BELA PORTRAIT

Opposite page: Painted by Geza Kende in 1932, this painting of Bela turned up practically in my own backyard, only for me to purchase it years later in an auction.

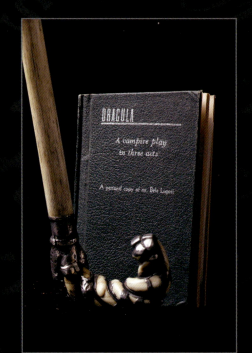

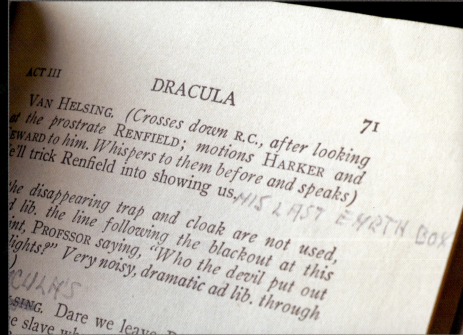

ACT III

DRACULA

71

VAN HELSING. (Crosses down R.C., after looking at the prostrate RENFIELD; motions HARKER and EWARD to him. Whispers to them before and speaks) e'll trick Renfield into showing us. HIS LAST EARTH BOX

he disappearing trap and cloak are not used, d lib. the line following the blackout at this int, PROFSSOR saying, "Who the devil put out lights?" Very noisy, dramatic ad lib. through

CULA'S

LSING. Dare we leave e slave wh